Food & Nutrition Sciences
LAB MANUAL

First Canadian Edition

Authors
Michelyn Putignano
Family Studies Department Head
Delta Secondary School
Hamilton District School Board

Karen Wilson
Family Studies Department Head
Westdale Secondary School
Hamilton District School Board

McGraw-Hill Ryerson

McGraw-Hill Ryerson
Toronto Montréal Boston Burr Ridge, IL Dubuque, IA Madison, WI New York San Francisco St. Louis Bangkok Bogotá Caracas Kuala Lumpur Lisbon London Madrid Mexico City Milan New Delhi Santiago Seoul Singapore Sydney Taipei

COPIES OF THIS BOOK MAY BE OBTAINED BY CONTACTING:

McGraw-Hill Ryerson Ltd.

WEB SITE:
http://www.mcgrawhill.ca

E-MAIL:
orders@mcgrawhill.ca

TOLL-FREE FAX:
1-800-463-5885

TOLL-FREE CALL:
1-800-565-5758

OR BY MAILING YOUR ORDER TO:
McGraw-Hill Ryerson
Order Department
300 Water Street
Whitby, ON L1N 9B6

Please quote the ISBN and title when placing your order.

ISBN: 0-07-095238-8

The McGraw-Hill Companies

McGraw-Hill Ryerson

Food and Nutrition Sciences Lab Manual

ISBN 0-07-095238-8

http://www.mcgrawhill.ca

1 2 3 4 5 6 7 8 9 10 TRI 0 9 8 7 6 5

Printed and bound in Canada

Care has been taken to trace ownership of copyright material contained in this text. The publishers will gladly accept any information that will enable them to rectify any reference or credit in subsequent printings.

National Library of Canada Cataloging in Publication Data
Putignano, Michelyn
Food and nutrition sciences lab manual / Michelyn Putignano, Karen Wilson.1st —Canadian ed.

ISBN 0-07-095238-8

1. Nutrition—Laboratory manuals. 2. Food—Laboratory manuals.
I. Wilson, Karen II. Title.

TX364.P87 2004 613.2'078 C2004-904255-6

PUBLISHER: Patty Pappas
SPONSORING Editor: Debbie Davidson
PROJECT MANAGER/DEVELOPMENTAL EDITOR: Ellen Munro
MANAGER, EDITORIAL SERVICES: Linda Allison
SUPERVISING EDITOR: Kristi Moreau
EDITORIAL COORDINATOR: Valerie Janicki
COPY EDITOR: Karen Rolfe
PERMISSIONS EDITOR: Paula Joiner
EDITORIAL ASSISTANT: Erin Hartley
MANAGER, PRODUCTION SERVICES: Yolanda Pigden
SENIOR PRODUCTION COORDINATOR: Jennifer Wilkie
COVER DESIGN: Dianna Little
ELECTRONIC PAGE MAKE-UP: Jay Tee Graphics Ltd.

Advisory Team

Student Success
David Chambers
School to Work, Successful Pathways Coordinator
Durham District School Board

Character Education
Marc Kierstead
Secondary Consultant
York Catholic District School Board

Assessment and Evaluation
Garfield Gini-Newman
Instructor
Ontario Institute for Studies in Education
University of Toronto

Literacy
Cathy Costello
Curriculum Co-coordinator, Literacy
York Region District School Board

Career Education
Judi Misener
Principal, Sir William Osler High School
Toronto District School Board

Food Specialist
Lesia Hucal
Registered Dietitian
Hamilton Ontario

Reviewers

Patricia Andres
Family Studies Department Head
Eden High School
District School Board of Niagara

Gwenne August
Assistant Curriculum Leader, Family Studies
Albert Campbell Collegiate
Toronto District School Board

Jennifer George Malkovich
Consultant
Hamilton Wentworth District School Board

Ingrid Geppert
Family Studies Teacher
Gloucester High School
Ottawa-Carlton District School Board

Urmil Gupta
Teacher
Marc Garneau Collegiate Institute
Toronto District School Board

Victoria Houston
Teacher
Century Secondary School
Greater Essex County District School Board

Erika Leslie
Family Studies Teacher
Peel District School Board

Ann McClure
Curriculum Consultant
Simcoe District School Board

Diane O'Shea
Family Studies Department
Medway High School
Thames Valley District School Board

Diana Smith
Head of Family Studies
Pierre Elliott Trudeau High School
York Region District School Board

Laurie Spittles
Teacher
The Woodlands School
Peel District School Board

Linda Triantafillou
Curriculum Consultant
Halton Catholic District School Board

Anne Wibberley
Brantford Collegiate Institute
Greater Essex District School Board

Contents

Introduction: To the Student

Using the *Food and Nutrition Sciences Lab Manual* with *Food for Today, First Canadian Edition*

This manual has been designed to be used with the text, *Food for Today, First Canadian Edition.* Unit overviews have been provided to show you how the text can be used as an integral part of the Grade 12 course *Food and Nutrition Sciences*. Unit 6 of *Food for Today* was specifically designed to address the expectations of that course. *Food for Today, First Canadian Edition* provides a unique Canadian perspective on food and nutrition that is not available anywhere else. Unit 6 helps students understand the nutritional status of Canadians, current trends in food preparation, world cuisine, the factors affecting Canadian food production and supply, and issues relating to food security and hunger on a worldwide basis. The remainder of the text can be used to supplement course materials.

What's in the *Food and Nutrition Sciences Lab Manual*?

You will find a number of different types of activities within this manual. Each unit contains:

- **Unit Planners:** Each is an overview of the content covered in the unit.
- **Diagnostic Tests:** Allow you to see what you know prior to beginning the unit.
- **Study Guides:** A variety of question types is provided to help you review what you have learned.
- **Unit Culminating Activity:** Covers the key material learned in the unit. An assessment tool is provided for each unit's Culminating Activity.
- **Course Culminating Activity:** Divided into four phases. You will complete one phase at the end of each unit. A detailed evaluation is provided for each phase.
- **Food Labs:** The labs show you the practical applications of the course theoretical knowledge.
- **Course Activities:** These are learning opportunities in the areas of social science research, literacy, and careers in the social sciences. Additional activities reinforce learning about issues in food and nutrition sciences.

Course Culminating Activity

The course Culminating Activity has been divided into four phases. One phase will be completed at the end of each unit. You will work as part of a marketing team to design, create, and market a new and innovative food product based on research conducted to identify a need in the marketplace.

The Culminating Activity will be divided as follows:

- **Unit One—Identify a Product**
  Your team will identify a product that you would like to produce and market, based on an initial investigation of the current marketplace. You and your team will identify and determine who will use your product and why your product is needed.
- **Unit Two—Market Research**
  Your team will conduct primary research to determine the needs of the marketplace and how those needs can best be addressed in a food product.

- **Unit Three—Designing the Product**
  During Phase Three your team will analyse the data collected during the research phase to begin to create your product. You will conduct a test run and make any revisions necessary for a successful result. You will also need to identify the source of the ingredients and any ethical issues related to the production of the product..
- **Unit Four—Production and Marketing**
  In the final phase you will produce and market the final product. You will need to design your packaging and distribute your product. You will also evaluate the success of your project.

You will find the Culminating Activity and assessment tools at the end of the manual.

Introduction: To the Teacher

Food for Today and the *Food and Nutrition Sciences* Lab Manual

Food for Today, First Canadian Edition, was written initially to address the expectations for the Grade 9/10 course *Food and Nutrition* (HFN10/20). The unit overviews show how this text can also be used as an integral part of the Grade 12 course *Food and Nutrition Sciences*. In fact, Unit 6 of *Food for Today* was specifically designed to address the expectations of this Grade 12 course on healthy living. *Food for Today, First Canadian Edition* provides a unique Canadian perspective on food and nutrition that is not available anywhere else. This unit helps students understand the nutritional status of Canadians, current trends in food preparation, world cuisine, the factors affecting Canadian food production and supply, and issues relating to food security and hunger on a worldwide basis.

What's in the *Food and Nutrition Sciences Manual*?

The manual has been divided into four units to correspond to the *Food and Nutrition* course profile (http://www.curriculum.org/occ/profiles/12/social_p.shtml). The unit overview charts allow you to identify the corresponding sections of *Food for Today, First Canadian Edition.*

Test questions are provided in each unit, and answers are given, where appropriate. You will find a number of different types of activities within this manual. In detail, each manual contains:

- **Unit Planner:** An overview of the content covered in the unit.
- **Diagnostic Test:** Allows students to assess what they know prior to beginning the unit.
- **Study Guides:** A variety of question types is provided to help students review what they have learned.
- **Unit Culminating Activity:** Covers the key material in the unit. An assessment tool is provided for each unit's Culminating Activity.
- **Course Culminating Activity:** Divided into four phases. Students will complete one phase at the end of each unit. A detailed evaluation is provided for each phase.
- **Food Labs:** Teach students the practical applications of the course theoretical knowledge.
- **Course Activities:** Learning opportunities in the areas of social science research, literacy, and careers in social science. Additional activities reinforce learning about issues in food and nutrition sciences.

Course Culminating Activity

The course Culminating Activity has been divided into four phases. One phase will be completed at the end of each unit. Students will work as part of a marketing team to design, create, and market a new and innovative food product based on research conducted to identify a need in the marketplace. The teacher may choose to use portions of a video such as *Daddy Day Care* (2002) or *Baby Boom* (1987) to introduce the concept of market research.

The Culminating Activity will be divided as follows:

- **Unit One—Identify a Product**
  Your team will identify a product that they would like to produce and market, based on an initial investigation of the current marketplace. You and your team will identify and determine who will use your product and why your product is needed.
- **Unit Two—Market Research**
  Your team will conduct primary research to determine the needs of the marketplace and how those needs can best be addressed in a food product.
- **Unit Three—Designing the Product**
  During Phase Three your team will analyse the data collected during the research phase to begin to create your product. You will conduct a test run and make any revisions necessary. You will also need to identify the source of the ingredients and any ethical issues related to the production of the product.
- **Unit Four—Production and Marketing**
  In the final phase you will produce and market the final product. You will need to design your packaging and distribute your product. You will also evaluate the success of your project.

You will find the Culminating Activity and assessment tools at the end of the student manual.

Name: ______________________ Date: __________ Class: __________

Unit 1: Nutrition and Well-being

1-1

What You Need to Know	Where to Find It
■ Factors affecting eating habits with specific emphasis on the most basic reason for eating — survival.	■ Ch. 1: Our Food Needs (pp. 3–7)
■ The role of nutrients and how they are used by the body. ■ The impact on health when nutritional needs are not met.	■ Ch. 11: Nutrient Wise ◦ Nutrients (pp. 223–226) ◦ How Your Body Uses Food (pp. 249–252) ◦ Carbohydrates, Fibre, and Proteins (pp. 229–234) ◦ Fats (pp. 234–238) ◦ Micronutrients (pp. 238–248)
■ The role and message of *Canada's Food Guide to Healthy Eating* and other food guidelines in relation to recommended nutrient intakes.	■ Ch. 11: Nutrient Wise ◦ What Is the Purpose of Dietary Reference Intakes? (pp. 226–228) ■ Ch. 12: Nutritious Meals ◦ *Canada's Guidelines for Healthy Eating* (pp. 265–270) ◦ *Canada's Food Guide to Healthy Eating* (pp. 271–280) ◦ The Purpose of Food Guides (pp. 273–280)
■ Energy balance.	■ Ch. 19: Achieving a Healthy Body Weight ◦ Maintaining Healthy Weight (pp. 393–394) ◦ Body-Weight Classification (pp. 394–396) ◦ Limitations with the Body-Weight Classification System (pp. 396–400) ◦ Weight Management (pages 400–406) ■ Ch. 20: Reducing Fat in Your Diet (pp. 411–426)—optional ■ Ch. 21: Strategies for Achieving Well-Being (pp. 431–445)—optional
■ Conducting Social Science research.	■ The Social Science Research Process (p. 13) ■ Developing Research Skills Using Internet Sources (p. 600)
■ Unit review.	■ Ch. 28: Nutritional Status of Canadians (pp. 581–600)
■ Food labs applying scientific principles related to nutrients, food preparation, and storage.	■ Food labs or activities ◦ Fat lab (similar to Making Invisible Fats Visible on p. 418) ◦ Sugar lab ◦ Starch lab ◦ Muffins and smoothies ◦ Making breakfast count
■ Unit Culminating Activity: Analysis of students' diets compared to the recommended nutrient intakes of Canadian males and females.	

Name: ______________________ Date: __________ Class: __________

1-2 **DIAGNOSTIC QUIZ**

Unit 1: Nutrition Essentials for Health and Well-Being

Multiple Choice

For each of the following questions, circle the letter of the most appropriate answer.

1. Fat has approximately ________________ the calories per gram as carbohydrates.
a. $^1/_2$ **c.** 2 times
b. $^1/_4$ **d.** 10 times

2. The function of carbohydrates is:
a. To protect the body's vital organs.
b. To build and repair cells.
c. To help chemical reactions in the body.
d. To provide the body's main source of energy.

3. Protein is made up of:
a. Amino acids joined together.
b. Sugars joined together.
c. Fats joined together.
d. Vitamins and minerals joined together.

4. Which statement best describes the process of digestion?
a. The breakdown of food into simpler substances for the body to use.
b. The collection of waste products that result from digestion.
c. The passage of food from the digestive tract into the circulatory system.
d. The transportation of nutrients and oxygen to individual body cells.

5. About how long is the digestive tract, from beginning to end?
a. 10 cm. **c.** 10 m
b. 2 m. **d.** 25 m.

6. A main nutrient that does not provide energy is:
a. Vitamins. **c.** Protein.
b. Carbohydrates. **d.** Fat.

7. Which of the following best describes the pathway of food in the digestion process?
a. Esophagus, stomach, small intestine.
b. Large intestine, stomach, esophagus.
c. Mouth, stomach, esophagus.
d. Stomach, small intestine, esophagus.

8. Which part of the small intestine increases the surface area of absorption?
a. Capillaries.
b. Duodenum.
c. Colon.
d. Villi.

9. How many servings of vegetables and fruits a day does *Canada's Food Guide to Healthy Eating* suggest that people should have?
a. 1.
b. 2–3.
c. 5–10.
d. 10–15.

10. The best way to describe the average Canadian diet is:
a. High in fats, cholesterol, and sugar.
b. High in nutrients from vegetables.
c. High in vitamins, minerals, and fibre.
d. Low in sodium.

11. According to dietary guidelines, limiting salt and sodium in the diet may help reduce the risk of:
a. Cancer.
b. High blood pressure.
c. Obesity.
d. Tooth decay.

Short Answer

Fill in the following answers. If you do not know the answer, speculate about what you think it might be.

12. What is the purpose of the Dietary Reference Intakes?

____

____

13. List the six main nutrients. Indicate whether they are macronutrients or micronutrients and whether they are a source of energy or not.

Nutrient	Macro or Micro?	Energy Source (Yes or No?)
1.		
2.		
3.		
4.		
5.		
6.		

14. List three eating habits that promote normal digestion and absorption.

____

____

____

15. Give two examples of how inadequate nutrition may contribute to a decreased state of wellness.

____

____

____

____

16. Describe how dietitians use patient food diaries.

____

____

____

____

____

Name: ______________________ Date: __________ Class: __________

STUDY GUIDE **1-3**

Nutrients

Use pages 223–248 of *Food for Today, First Canadian Edition*, to answer the following questions.

Knowledge and Understanding

1. Define the following terms and give examples.

Nutrient deficiency	
Malnutrition	
Low-income cut-offs	
Calorie	
Essential amino acids	
Cholesterol	
Hydrogenation	
Antioxidants	
Electrolytes	

2. a. How much energy is provided in each of the main nutrients?

b. Carbohydrates have ______ calories/gram.

c. Proteins have _______ calories/gram.

d. Fat has _______ calories/gram.

Thinking and Inquiry

3. The nutrition information on a granola bar label indicates it has 4 g of protein, 9 g of fat, and 32 g of carbohydrate. Calculate how much energy is provided by the granola bar.

____

____

____

____

4. Nutrition experts recommend that people generally obtain how many calories from food?

a. Carbohydrates: _____ percent per day

b. Fat: No more than _____ percent per day

c. Protein: _____ percent per day.

5. The nutrition information on a yogurt label reveals that it has 5 g of protein, 5 g of fat, and 20 g of carbohydrates. Calculate the percentage of fat to determine if this yogurt falls within the daily recommendation for fat.

____

____

____

____

Carbohydrates

6. List the three main sources of carbohydrates.

____

____

____

Fibre

7. a. Describe the two types of fibre.

____

____

____

____

b. Calculate how much fibre you should consume a day.

______

______

Proteins

8. What are the functions of protein in the body?

______

______

9. What are sources of complete and incomplete proteins?

a. Complete proteins: ______

______

b. Incomplete proteins: ______

______

Fats

10. List four functions of fats in the body.

______

______

______

______

11. What are the risks of consuming too much fat?

______

______

Cholesterol, Fats, and Health

12. Describe the differences between LDL and HDL cholesterol.

LDL ______

______

HDL ______

______

13. State whether each of the following contains saturated, polyunsaturated, or monounsaturated fat.

a. Soybean oil: ______________________

b. Olive oil: ______________________

c. Chicken: ______________________

d. Butter: ______________________

e. Safflower margarine: ______________________

f. Homogenized milk: ______________________

14. How do trans fats affect health?

____

____

Vitamins

15. Fill in the spaces in the chart below with information about vitamins.

Vitamin	Information
	■ Citrus fruits are good sources of this vitamin.
Vitamin D	
	■ Helps build red blood cells and form genetic material. ■ Helps prevent birth defects (needed by women trying to get pregnant or who are pregnant).
Vitamin E	
	■ Helps the body release energy from carbohydrates, fats, and proteins.
Vitamin A	
	■ Helps the blood clot normally.

Minerals

16. Fill in the spaces in the chart below with information about minerals.

Mineral	Information
	■ A lack of this mineral may lead to osteoporosis.
Fluoride	
	■ Helps carry oxygen in the blood.
Phosphorus	
	■ Helps build bone and make protein. ■ Helps nerves and muscles work normally.
Iodine	
	■ Helps the body heal wounds and form blood. ■ Affects the senses of taste and smell.
Sodium	
	■ Helps maintain the heartbeat. ■ Bananas are a good source of this mineral.

Water

17. Describe the functions of water in the body.

____

____

____

____

____

____

Name: ______________________ Date: __________ Class: __________

1-4

STUDY GUIDE

Applying Your Knowledge About Nutrients

Thinking and Inquiry, Communication, Application

1. For each situation, find the error in thinking. Then explain why the person's reasoning is wrong.
   a. When Natasha discovered that her blood cholesterol was high, she decided to eliminate some of her favourite foods, including peanut butter and olive oil, from her cooking.

   b. Some of Praveen's friends have suggested taking a vitamin and mineral supplement. Recently, Jordan has started taking three or four vitamin pills a day, thinking, "If a little is good, a lot would be better."

   c. In an effort to lose weight, Graeme has started a new low-carbohydrate diet. Bread, pasta, and rice are not allowed and most fruits are prohibited. He doesn't mind all that much, since he gets to eat all the meat he wants.

d. Andre is thinking of becoming a vegetarian, but he is not sure because he weight trains. He is concerned that without meat he won't get enough protein to work into his training to build more muscle.

____

____

____

____

____

2. Complete the following chart.

Food	Fibre (Yes or No?)	Complete or Incomplete Protein	Cholesterol (Yes or No?)
Eggs			
Chick peas			
Peanut butter			
Fish			
Vegetable oil			
Butter			
Soy			
Liver			
Margarine			
Spinach			

3. Use the space provided to write your main argument. Then, on a separate sheet of paper, write a complete response.

A few years ago, many foods, including potato chips, crackers, and peanut butter advertised that they did not contain **cholesterol**. Many companies are now advertising their products as low in (or not containing) **trans fats**. Describe what this means and what impact it may have on the products.

____

____

____

____

____

____

4. How does poverty affect the nutritional status of people?

____

____

____

____

____

____

5. Many runners, bicyclists, soccer players, and other athletes consume special drinks before, during, or after strenuous exercise. Why do athletes consume these drinks? What do they do?

____

____

____

____

____

____

____

Name: ______________________ Date: __________ Class: __________

Energy Input—How Does This Day Compare?

- For the following food diary, calculate the total nutrients that would be consumed.
- Next, compare your results to the nutrient requirements of an adolescent female 14–18 years of age. (See Resources for Energy Input and Output, Reference 2, at the back of this manual.) Note the comparison to DRIs and ULs. You may also refer to Chapter 28: Nutritional Status of Canadians in *Food for Today, First Canadian Edition*, to compare (with a focus on pages 593 and 596).
- You may use the Nutrient Calculation Worksheet (Reference 3) at the back of this manual to help you complete this task. It provides a number of ways to access nutrient information data.
- Make suggestions for an improved diet.

Chandra's Food Diary

Breakfast

- Nothing. It's too early to eat!

Upon arrival to school

- Okay, now I'm getting a little hungry after walking to school!
- 250 ml hot chocolate from the machine in the caf. It's made from powder, but it tastes pretty good.
- 1 bagel (toasted).
- 1 pat of butter (about 5 ml).

During break

1 medium-size orange. It tides me over until lunch.

Lunch

- Medium French fries (about 20 fries). I thought I would go for something else, but they looked so good.
- Gravy for taste (about 15 ml). You see them making it in the morning from a powder.
- Ketchup for dipping (about 5 ml).
- Bottle of Coke or Pepsi (about 500 ml). It's one of those biggish bottles.

After school

- Glass of 2% milk (about 250 ml).
- Peanut butter and jam sandwich—2 slices of whole wheat bread—that's all that there is in the house—30 ml of peanut butter—I like it thick—and about 15 ml of my favourite raspberry jam.

Off to Work

- Nothing but a glass of water (about 250 ml).

Supper

I reheated it because it has been left for me.

- Chicken breast, roasted (1 full piece).
- Homemade mashed potatoes (125 ml scoop).
- 250 ml boiled baby carrots.
- Apple juice (250 ml).

How could Chandra improve her diet?

Name: ______________________ Date: __________ Class: __________

FOOD LAB **1-6**

Detecting the Presence of Fat in Food

Fat is present in a variety of foods. Sometimes it is very visible, such as in oil or butter or in the marbling in meat. Other times, you cannot see it, so you may not even be aware of it. These fats are called invisible fats.

Purpose

To investigate the presence of fat in various food products.

Materials

8 foods
Paper (e.g., paper towel, brown bag, writing paper)

Method

1. Using the same type of paper consistently throughout the experiment, smear a small amount of the food on a piece of paper.
2. Wipe off the food so there is no residue.
3. Let the paper dry for about a half hour then make your observations.

Observations

Complete the chart below using the foods your group has selected. If the substance turns the paper translucent (or slightly see-through), it contains fat. If it dries to the original colour of the paper (and opaque), it does not contain fat.

FOOD		PAPER		CONCLUSION
Item	**Description**	**How It Affects the Paper Immediately**	**How It Affects the Paper After 30 Minutes**	**Does It Contain Fat?**
1.				
2.				
3.				
4.				

Name: ______________________ Date: __________ Class: __________

1-6 FOOD LAB—DETECTING THE PRESENCE OF FAT IN FOOD, *continued*

FOOD		PAPER		CONCLUSION
Item	**Description**	**How It affects the Paper Immediately**	**How It Affects the Paper After 30 Minutes**	**Does It Contain Fat?**
5.				
6.				
7.				
8.				

Questions

1. Why are fats needed in the body?

2. Why are fats a concern when eaten in excess amounts?

3. This experiment tests only for the presence of fat; it does not differentiate between types of fats. From the foods you chose, determine saturated versus unsaturated fats and whether the product has been hydrogenated or not. Give reasons for your conclusions.

Name: ______________________ Date: __________ Class: __________

FOOD LAB 1-7

Testing for Simple Sugars

Simple sugars are part of the ______________________ group of nutrients. They are the basic unit that ultimately will be turned into ______________________ (a type of sugar) and then converted into ______________________ for storage in the body's cells.

Purpose

To investigate the presence of simple sugars in various food products.

Materials

Frying pan with lid
6 glasses
Water
6 food products (choose from grain products, milk products, and fruits or vegetables)
Benedict's Solution

Method

1. Use an electric frying pan as a hot water bath. To do this, fill the electric frying pan with about 1 cm of water. Place the lid on and warm the water. (Watch over the frying pan when it is in use.)
2. Place foods in separate glasses.
   - If the food is a liquid, pour enough to just cover the bottom of the glass.
   - If the food is a solid (e.g., banana, apple, potato chips), crush a small amount and add enough water to cover the bottom of the glass.
3. Add 10 drops of Benedict's Solution to each glass.
4. Place the glasses in the hot water bath and note your observations.

Alternatively, this may be done using test tubes and a Bunsen burner to slowly heat the contents.

Observations

Complete the chart below using the foods your group has compiled. The Benedict's Solution provides a test for the presence of simple sugars. If sugar is present, the Benedict's Solution will turn colour (shades of yellow, orange, brown).

Food Product	Description of Any Change(s) Before Heating	Description of Any Change(s) After Heating	Conclusion: Are Simple Sugars Present?
1.			
2.			
3.			
4.			
5.			
6.			

FOOD LAB—TESTING FOR SIMPLE SUGARS, *continued*

Questions

1. Why does some food need to be crushed?

2. Why do the colours intensify with the continued application of heat?

3. There are probably different kinds of simple sugars present in the foods you tested. For each of your foods used, determine what sugars are present. You may refer to *Food for Today, First Canadian Edition*, pages 231–232, for information about the different forms of sugars.

-
-
-
-
-

Name: ______________________ Date: __________ Class: __________

1-8 **FOOD LAB**

Detecting the Presence of Starch in Food

Starch is part of the ____________________ group of nutrients. It is ____________________ because many sugars are ________________________ together. In digestion, it is one of the first nutrients to be broken down. The enzyme ________________________ breaks the bonds of starch to produce simpler ________________________.

Purpose

To investigate the presence of starch in various food products.

Materials

Plate
8 different food products (use grain products, fruits, and vegetables)
Iodine solution

Method

1. Place a sample of each food on the plate. Test similar amounts of each food.
2. Place a few drops of iodine solution on each food.
3. Make observations immediately.
4. Wait a few more minutes and note any other changes.

Name: ______________________ Date: __________ Class: __________

FOOD LAB—DETECTING THE PRESENCE OF STARCH IN FOOD, *continued*

1-8

Observations

Complete the chart below using the foods your group has compiled. When drops of iodine solution are applied to a food containing starch, the solution will turn dark blue, purple, or blackish.

Food Product	Description Before Testing	Description After Testing	Conclusion Are Simple Sugars Present?
1.			
2.			
3.			
4.			
5.			
6.			
7.			
8.			

Name: ______________________ Date: __________ Class: __________

Questions

1. Many experiments have controls. What can be used as a control? Why is it ideal to have a control?

2. Icing sugar tests positive for starch. Why?

3. Starchy foods are often discouraged in many low-carbohydrate and/or high-protein diets. Find information about one of these diets and describe the foods discouraged in it.

4. Why should people be wary of low-carbohydrate and/or high-protein diets?

Name: ______________________ Date: __________ Class: __________

STUDY GUIDE 1-9

How the Body Uses Food

Use *Food for Today, First Canadian Edition*, pages 249–251, to answer the following questions.

Knowledge and Understanding

1. Define the following terms.

Peristalsis	
Chyme	
Bile	
Glucose	
Villi	
Liver	
Glycogen	
Oxidation	

Name: ______________________ Date: __________ Class: __________

2. For each number, name the part of the digestive process and describe what happens.

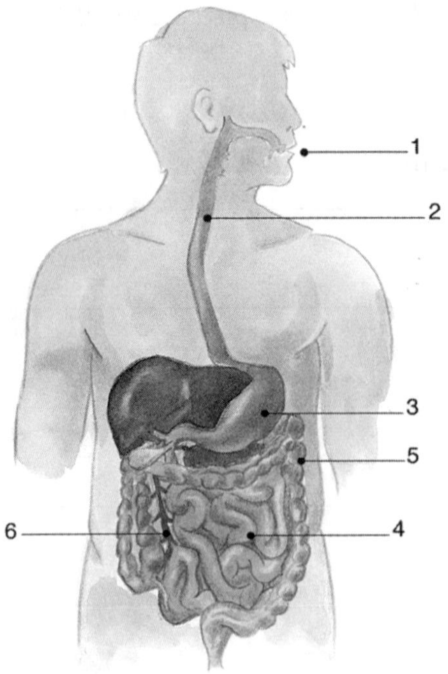

Body Part	What Happens to Food
1.	
2.	
3.	
4.	
5.	
6.	

STUDY GUIDE—HOW THE BODY USES FOOD, *continued*

3. How long does it take each of the main nutrients to leave the stomach?
   a. Carbohydrates

   b. Proteins

   c. Fats

4. Fully describe the purposes for which the body needs energy.

   ____
   ____
   ____
   ____
   ____
   ____
   ____
   ____

5. Basal metabolism rate depends on:

   - ____________________
   - ____________________
   - ____________________

Thinking and Inquiry

Answer the following on a separate sheet of paper.

6. Fibre is considered necessary for the body, although it does not provide any nutrients or energy. Describe why fibre is necessary for the digestive system.

7. Gall bladder disease is a common problem, especially among women who are somewhat overweight. Describe gall bladder disease and how it is treated.

8. Some people have fast metabolisms while other people have slow metabolisms. Describe how a person may alter his or her metabolism.

Name: ______________________ Date: __________ Class: __________

1-10 **FOOD LAB**

Digestion

Specific Expectations

- Plan a menu for, select, and prepare foods that meet selected dietary needs during the different stages of life.
- Identify the source of nutrients and the role they play in the maintenance of good health.
- Identify the role of fibre and water in the body, and the sources and roles of the major components of nutrients (e.g., carbohydrates, fats, proteins, vitamins, minerals).
- Demonstrate an understanding of the nutrients provided by foods in each category of *Canada's Food Guide to Healthy Eating* and other dietary guides and standards and, using this knowledge, describe ways to achieve healthy body weight and body image.
- Report information gathered from an existing database on the processes of digestion, absorption, and metabolism of food, and on the caloric intake of individuals.
- Correctly use the terminology of food and nutrition sciences.
- Effectively communicate the results of your inquiries.

You will design a snack and a smoothie that are tasty and packed with nutrients.

1. Choose or design a smoothie recipe.
2. Choose a recipe for a muffin, snack bar, or energy bar that incorporates some additional nutrients, most notably fibre. The recipe itself may be nutrient-dense and/or you may add or alter the recipe to make it more nutritious.

When you hand in the assignment:

- Provide a copy of the recipe for the smoothie.
- Provide a copy of the recipe for the snack.
- Design and fill in all the charts.
- Answer all the questions.

Assignment

1. Develop a chart that clearly shows the main ingredients in your smoothie and snack. All ingredients should be listed for the smoothie, but only the main ingredients should be listed for the snack—not salt, baking soda or powder, or spices.

FOOD LAB—DIGESTION, *continued*

2. Using the list of main ingredients from Step 1 and information from *Food for Today, First Canadian Edition*, and your class, identify the main nutrients in your products. Identify the functions of these nutrients for the body. Concentrate on identifying the main macronutrients (carbohydrates, protein, and fat), and one or two micronutrients (specific vitamins and/or minerals) for each ingredient.

   For example, you may use a chart as follows:

Ingredient	Nutrient(s) Present	Function(s) of Nutrient

3. Using your ingredients list again, note the amount of each ingredient. Then, using a nutrient table, analyse the nutritional value of your smoothie and snack. You may use the chart provided or develop one yourself.
4. Using proper terminology, outline how each of the nutrients in your smoothie and snack is digested, absorbed, and metabolized during each stage of digestion. Use diagrams if needed. Be specific as to the ingredients in your smoothie and snack and to the stages and steps of digestion.
5. Discuss the following questions:
   - **a.** How did you or could you increase the fibre content of your smoothie and snack?
   - **b.** What is the role of fibre in the body?
   - **c.** Is water present in your snack? If so, in what form? What is the role of water in the body?
   - **d.** How can this recipe be incorporated into a healthy diet that promotes a healthy body weight or body image? Consider the findings of your nutrient analysis table in Step 2. Would any ingredients need to be replaced, added, or altered? If so, which ones?

Name: ____________________ Date: __________ Class: __________

1-10

Nutrient Values of Main Ingredients

Smoothie						
Ingredient	**Amount Used in Your Recipe** *Conversion Needed	**Calories (kcals)**	**Carbohydrates (grams)**	**Fibre (grams)**	**Protein (grams)**	**Fat (grams)**
Totals						

Snack						
Ingredient	**Amount Used in Your Recipe** *Conversion Needed	**Calories (kcals)**	**Carbohydrates (grams)**	**Fibre (grams)**	**Protein (grams)**	**Fat (grams)**
Totals						

Name: ______________________ Date: __________ Class: __________

FOOD LAB—DIGESTION, *continued*

1-10

Category/Expectations	Criteria	Level 1	Level 2	Level 3	Level 4
Knowledge and Understanding ■ Identify the role of fibre and water in the body, and the sources and roles of major components of nutrients. ■ Identify the source of nutrients and the role they play in the maintenance of good health.	■ Identifies the roles of fibre and water in the body (Step 5). ■ Identifies the food sources of a variety of nutrients (Step 2). ■ Identifies the functions of the nutrients from the chosen ingredients (Step 2).				
Thinking and Inquiry ■ Report information gathered from an existing database on the process of digestion, absorption, and metabolism of food, and on the caloric intake of individuals.	■ Identifies the digestive, absorption, and metabolic process for the major nutrients—carbohydrates, proteins, and fat—for specific recipe (Step 4 written and diagram).				
Communication ■ Correctly use the terminology of food and nutrition sciences. ■ Effectively communicate the results of your inquiries.	■ Uses correct terminology in charts and answers (steps 1–3 charts, steps 4–5 written and diagrams) ■ Presents report in complete, neat, organized, and creative manner.				
Application ■ Demonstrate an understanding of the nutrients in guidelines and standards, and use this knowledge to describe ways to achieve a healthy body weight and body image.	■ Forms conclusions regarding common nutrient values of food (Step 3 chart and Step 5 questions). ■ Explains how the recipe could be incorporated into a healthy diet that promotes a healthy body weight and body image (recipe choices and Step 5 questions).				

Name: ______________________ Date: __________ Class: __________

1-11 **STUDY GUIDE**

Canada's Guidelines for Healthy Eating

Use *Food for Today, First Canadian Edition*, pages 265–281, to answer the following questions.

Knowledge and Understanding

Canada's Guidelines for Healthy Eating

1. List five Canadian guidelines for healthy eating.

- ______________________
- ______________________
- ______________________
- ______________________
- ______________________

2. Why is it important to have a variety of foods?

____

____

3. Distinguish between visible and invisible fat.

____

____

____

____

4. Caffeine should be limited to ________ mg per day according to the Dietitians of Canada. This equals ________ cups of coffee per day. Other things that contain caffeine include ______________, ______________, and ______________.

5. Good nutrition is important in order to reduce the risk of developing nutrition-related diseases including:

- ______________________
- ______________________
- ______________________
- ______________________
- ______________________

Name: ______________________ Date: __________ Class: __________

STUDY GUIDE—*CANADA'S GUIDELINES FOR HEALTHY EATING, continued*

1-11

Canada's Food Guide to Healthy Eating

6. Fill in the following chart about *Canada's Food Guide to Healthy Eating*.

Food Group	Number of Servings	Sample Foods	Main Nutrients
Grains Products			
Vegetables and Fruits			
Milk and Milk Products			
Meat and Alternatives			

7. Why and how is the rainbow used as a tool for the food guide?

____

____

Other Foods

8. List five categories of "other" foods.

- ■ ____
- ■ ____
- ■ ____
- ■ ____
- ■ ____

9. What are the recommendations for "other" foods?

____

____

STUDY GUIDE—*CANADA'S GUIDELINES FOR HEALTHY EATING, continued*

Thinking and Inquiry

Answer the following questions on a separate sheet of paper.

10. Describe the messages that *Canada's Food Guide to Healthy Eating* and *Canada's Guidelines for Healthy Eating* give about "good" and "bad" foods.

11. Examine other food guides and explain how they show nutrient density without using a rainbow. (For food guides for different cultures, go to http://www.nal.usda.gov/fnic/etext/000023.html#xtocid2381818; for cultural adaptations of *Canada's Food Guide to Healthy Eating* go to http://www.nutritionrc.ca/guide.html.)

Name: ______________________ Date: __________ Class: __________

ISSUE

1-12

Canada's Food Guide to Healthy Eating to Undergo an Update

[March 10, 2004] **Health Minister Pierre Pettigrew today officially announced that Health Canada will undertake a revision to *Canada's Food Guide to Healthy Eating*.**

"*Canada's Food Guide to Healthy Eating* is at the core of the dietary guidance that the federal government provides to Canadians," said Minister Pettigrew. "We know from recent research that the current Food Guide continues to promote a pattern of eating that is scientifically sound. Health Canada will ensure the Food Guide continues to promote a pattern of eating that meets nutritional needs, promotes health, and minimizes the risk of nutrition-related chronic disease. However, our research also tells us that the Food Guide can be improved and made more meaningful to Canadians in making healthy eating choices."

Since the current Food Guide and related dietary guidance was released in the early 1990s, science about the relationship between diet and health has evolved. To ensure Health Canada's guidance is consistent with the latest science, the Department reviewed the Food Guide by consulting experts across the country.

The review included an assessment of diets which follow a pattern of eating recommended by the Food Guide. The review also assessed changes in the food supply and in eating patterns; an evaluation of the use and understanding of the food supply and in eating patterns; an evaluation of the use and understanding of the Food Guide by teachers, dietitians, public health personnel, and consumers; and a national stakeholder consultation.

Findings from the review have confirmed that the Food Guide remains a useful and valid tool for Canadians from both a scientific and an educational perspective. The review has confirmed the many strengths of the Food Guide, including its flexibility, simplicity, visual appeal, widespread awareness, and most importantly, its consistency with current science.

In spite of its many strengths, some challenges were identified when Canadians apply the guidance put forward by the Food Guide. For example, research has shown a lack of understanding of some of the terminology and messaging used, the need to modernize some elements, and a need to improve the promotion of the balanced approach to healthy eating that is the foundation of the Food Guide.

As such, over the next year, Health Canada will conduct further research and analysis on areas of a technical and communications nature to determine the extent of the updates that need to take place. Technical matters may include issues related to serving sizes, serving ranges, and the food groups. Communications matters may include issues related to terminology, target audiences, and graphics.

"It is clear that there is a great deal of support for the Food Guide and that it can continue to be used as the basis for providing and implementing healthy eating messages," said Dr. Carolyn Bennett, Minister of State (Public Health). "At the same time, however, undertaking a revision will provide an opportunity to work with stakeholders in response to the challenges that have been identified by Canadians."

The elements of the revision process are currently under development. The target for completion of the revision is in the Spring of 2006.

Questions

1. What are the goals of Health Canada in promoting *Canada's Food Guide to Healthy Eating*?

____

____

____

____

____

2. What kind of experts do you think would be involved with the revisions of *Canada's Food Guide to Healthy Eating*?

3. How was the review conducted?

4. Why do you think teachers, dietitians, and public health personnel were evaluated according to their understanding of *Canada's Food Guide to Healthy Eating*?

5. What are the strengths of the existing food guide?

6. What are the areas of improvement to be made?

7. Why might some Canadians be concerned about a review of *Canada's Food Guide to Healthy Eating*?

CANADA'S FOOD GUIDE TO HEALTHY EATING TO UNDERGO AN UPDATE, *continued*

8. How does Minister Pettigrew put the review in a positive light?

____

____

____

____

____

9. If you were a member of the consultant team reviewing *Canada's Food Guide to Healthy Eating*, how would you improve it? Consider the technical considerations (including serving size, serving ranges, and food groups) and the communications issues (terminology, target audience, and graphics). You may refer to additional web sites and outside information to assist you. (Comparison of international food guide pictorial representations go to: http://www.nal.usda.gov/fnic/etext/000023.html; for cultural Variations of *Canada's Food Guide to Healthy Eating* go to http://www.opha.on.ca/resources/foodguides.html.) Write your response on a separate sheet of paper.

Name: ______________________ Date: __________ Class: __________

1-13 **STUDY GUIDE**

Achieving a Healthy Body Weight

Use *Food for Today, First Canadian Edition*, pages 393–406, to answer the following questions.

Knowledge and Understanding

1. Define the following terms and give examples.

Set-point theory	
Waist-hip ratio	
Skinfold measure	
Fad diets	
Behavioural modification	

2. Factors that affect body weight include:

- ______________________
- ______________________
- ______________________
- ______________________

3. a. List common methods for determining weight.

____

____

____

____

b. Why are these methods not used for children?

____

____

4. Determine the Body Mass Index (BMI) and associated risks for the following people:

a. Toby is 25. He weighs 75 kg and is 195 cm tall.

Calculation of BMI
Associated risks

b. Antastasia is 37. She weighs 75 kg and is 163 cm tall.

Calculation of BMI
Associated risks

5. Why are BMI and waist circumference not always good indicators of a healthy weight?

____

____

____

____

6. Distinguish between apple- and pear-shaped people.

Apple	
Pear	

7. What are the advantages and disadvantages of measuring body-fat percentage?

____

____

____

8. List four approaches that are often used in fad diets.

- ■ ______________________
- ■ ______________________
- ■ ______________________
- ■ ______________________

9. How can exercise change your metabolism?

____

____

10. List three suggestions for those who want to gain weight.

- ■ ______________________
- ■ ______________________
- ■ ______________________

Thinking and Inquiry

Answer the following questions on a separate sheet of paper.

11. Waist circumference over specific measurement standards is considered hazardous to one's health. Similarly, having an apple shape is more of a health concern than having a pear shape. Why are diet-related health risks associated with these predictors of weight?

12. A university women's competitive swim team reported BMIs ranging from 27 to 30. Explain the validity or inaccuracy of the reading.

Name: ______________________ Date: __________ Class: __________

FOOD LAB **1-14**

Making Breakfast Count

Specific Expectations

- Identify the factors that affect personal food choices throughout the life cycle (e.g., age, health, school and/or work schedules, lifestyle, level of physical activity, lactation, special dietary needs).
- Plan a menu for, select, and prepare foods that meet selected dietary needs during the different stages of life.
- Identify the source of nutrients and the role they play in the maintenance of good health.
- Determine the relationship among nutrition, lifestyle, health, and disease.
- Demonstrate an understanding of the nutrients provided by foods in each category of *Canada's Food Guide to Healthy Eating* and other dietary guides and standards, and, using this knowledge, describe ways to achieve healthy body weight and body image.
- Demonstrate how to use equipment correctly to prepare and store foods for maximum nutrient retention.
- Effectively communicate the results of your inquiries, using a variety of methods and forms (e.g., graphs, charts, diagrams, oral presentations, written reports, videos).

Your Role

You are a dietitian working within a team to promote healthy breakfasts. You are responsible for helping people who do not normally eat breakfast to consider it. You will use your breakfast as an example of "Making Breakfast Count."

Target Group

- You must select a target group who do not usually eat breakfast. For example, it may be students who wake up late, parents who are getting their children ready for day care, or older individuals who live alone and just aren't hungry in the morning. Fully describe your target group and the reasons they don't eat breakfast.
- Alternatively, your target group may consist of people who eat breakfast but could make better choices.
- Explain why not eating breakfast could be hazardous to their health.

Advertising Your Message

- Using the slogan "Making Breakfast Count," develop an advertisement and/or public notice to grab their attention and make them want to eat breakfast. If you want to develop another slogan, you may.
- Describe to your target group why they should eat a healthy breakfast and the benefits of eating breakfast overall.

Making the Food

In your kitchen group, plan and prepare a simple breakfast or snack. It should be healthy and incorporate at least three of the food groups while recognizing the importance of the six main nutrients.

1. Make up a menu and have it checked by your teacher.
2. Fully explain how you will prepare the breakfast. You may use recipes and/or you may write down your own instructions.
3. List the equipment you will need to prepare the meal.
4. Provide your teacher with a list of required ingredients. Your teacher and your group will determine what is already on hand and what needs to be purchased and by whom.

Name: ______________________ Date: __________ Class: __________

Making Breakfast Count
Assessment and Evaluation

Category/Expectations	Criteria	Level 1	Level 2	Level 3	Level 4
Knowledge and Understanding ■ Identify the factors that affect personal food choices throughout the life cycle. ■ Demonstrate an understanding of the nutrients provided by foods in each category of *Canada's Food Guide to Healthy Eating* and other dietary guides and standards and, using this knowledge, describe ways to achieve healthy body weight and body image.	■ Identifies specific target group and the factors that affect their breakfast habits. ■ Advertisement and explanation help the target group recognize why a healthy breakfast is needed with a focus on: ◦ *Canada's Food Guide to Healthy Eating*. ◦ Main nutrients needed. ◦ Functions provided.				
Thinking and Inquiry ■ Identify the source of nutrients and the role they play in the maintenance of good health. ■ Determine the relationship among nutrition, lifestyle, health, and disease.	■ Connects the food made to the food groups, nutrients, and functions. ■ Connects the food made to the lifestyle of the specific target group and maintenance of health/prevention of disease.				
Communication ■ Effectively communicate the results of their inquiries, using a variety of methods and forms (e.g., graphs, charts, diagrams, oral presentations, written reports, videos).	■ Presents assignment in an organized manner. ■ Advertisement is suitably directed at target group. ■ Explanation is clear and concise.				
Application ■ Plan a menu for, select, and prepare foods that meet selected dietary needs during the different stages of life. ■ Demonstrate how to use equipment correctly to prepare and store foods for maximum nutrient retention.	■ Menu is planned. ■ Grocery list is provided and negotiated. ■ Equipment list is provided and negotiated. ■ Equipment is used correctly. ■ Menu and food are designed to maintain nutrients.				

Name: ____________________ Date: __________ Class: __________

1-15

REVIEW

Organizing Nutrients

Use the following list of nutrients and related words to create a mind map, web, or organizational chart. Each word should be used.

Macronutrients Soluble Calcium Provides energy Fats Incomplete Thiamin (B_1) Iodine D Microminerals Trans Carbohydrates Polyunsaturates Doesn't provide energy Simple sugars Insoluble E Magnesium Electrolytes Protein Cholesterol Folate (folacin or folic acid) Minerals Fat soluble B_{12} C Fluoride	Nutrients Complete Starches Amino acids Monounsaturates Fibre Copper Riboflavin (B_2) Chloride Vitamins A Micronutrients Pantothenic acid Saturates Zinc Sodium Biotin Bs Phosphorus Potassium Niacin (B_3) Iron K Water soluble B_6 Macrominerals Selenium

Name: ____________________ Date: __________ Class: __________

Not Quite Bill Nye the Science Guy

1-16

1. Review each of the tests you have done in class. For each, tell what procedure is used for testing and what a positive result is.

Test	How to Test?	Positive Result? How Do You Know?
Fat		
Simple sugars		
Complex sugars (starch)		

2. Consider the following foods. What would be their test results? If there is protein, is it complete (C) or incomplete (INC)?

Food	Fat (Yes or No?)	Simple Sugars (Yes or No?)	Starch (Yes or No?)	Protein (C / INC)
Chocolate milk				
Apple juice				
Salad dressing				
Macaroni and cheese (homemade)				
Protein shake				
Smart corn				
Fritos corn chips				
Croissant				
Tea biscuit				
Diet Sprite				
Sprite				
Gatorade				
V-8 juice				
Peanut butter and jam sandwich				
Cookie dough ice cream				
Milk chocolate bar				

Name: ______________________ Date: __________ Class: __________

1-17

Nutritional Status of Canadians

Answer the following questions on a separate sheet of paper, using *Food for Today, First Canadian Edition*, Chapter 28, pages 581–599. This serves as a review of the unit.

Thinking and Inquiry

1. The National Institute of Nutrition's 2001 Tracking Nutrition Trends Survey noted that Canadians rated their eating habits as very good to excellent (38 percent), good (42 percent), and fair to poor (20 percent).
   - **a.** How would this research be used?
   - **b.** How do these results compare with the dietitians' study?

2. Page 582 shows the ratings by age.
   - **a.** How is this useful?
   - **b.** Compare this research to the dietitians' study.

Communication

3. Using the information found in "Where Do Canadians Get Their Nutritional and Health Information?" on page 583:
   - **a.** Make a bar graph to display the information.
   - **b.** Comment on the validity of the overall picture.

4. Take notes about the information in "Factors Influencing Energy and Nutrient Needs" on page 586 to summarize what you have already learned from chapters 19 and 21.

5. Comment on the findings in "Are Canadians Eating Enough from the Four Food Groups?" on page 590.

6. Read "How Active Are Canadian Children?" on page 593. Provide three detailed suggestions on how to improve the activity levels of children (at school, home, etc.).

7. Summarize three main facts given about athletes in "Nutrient Needs of Athletes" on page 595.

Name: ______________________ Date: __________ Class: __________

Unit 1 Test Bank

Note: The teacher may use these questions to devise a test suitable to the exact content covered and the students' experiences. The questions may be given in a traditional test format and/or some indication of the questions could be given to students beforehand to facilitate additional research.

1. Which of the following is one of the six nutrient groups?
a. Chemicals.
b. Food groups.
c. Enzymes.
d. Carbohydrates.

2. Which of the following nutrients provides the greatest amount of energy?
a. 10 mg of vitamin C.
b. 10 g of carbohydrates.
c. 10 g of protein.
d. 10 g of fat.

3. Which statement best describes the digestion process?
a. Breakdown of food into simpler substances the body can use.
b. Collection of waste from the process.
c. Food passing from the digestive tract to the bloodstream.
d. Transporting chemicals to the cells of the body.

4. In which part of the digestive system does the least amount of digestion?
a. Esophagus.
b. Mouth.
c. Small intestine.
d. Stomach.

5. The substance that lines the stomach and protects it from the strong acid content is:
a. Bile.
b. Mucus.
c. Pancreatic juices.
d. Phytochemicals.

6. Which main nutrients are broken down in the mouth?
a. Sugars.
b. Fats.
c. Proteins.
d. Water.

7. Which main nutrients are broken down in the stomach?
a, Sugars.
b. Fats.
c. Proteins.
d. Water.

8. Carbohydrates are broken down during digestion into which basic units?
a. Amino acids.
b. Fatty acids.
c. Glycerols.
d. Simple sugars.

9. The part of the small intestine that increases surface area is:
a. Phytochemicals.
b. Mucus.
c. Duodenum.
d. Villi.

10. A person is most likely to feel full after eating a meal high in:
a. Vitamins. **c.** Simple sugars.
b. Fats. **d.** Water.

11. Which of the following is not a good source of fibre?
a. Chicken. **c.** Popcorn.
b. Lentils. **d.** Apple.

12. Which carbohydrate provides the most insoluble and soluble bulk in the diet?
a. Fibre. **c.** Sugar.
b. Fructose. **d.** Starch.

13. A build-up of plaque in arteries leading to the brain may result in:
a. Heart attack. **c.** Diabetes.
b. Stroke. **d.** High blood pressure.

14. Which of the following functions of protein can also be performed by carbohydrates and fats?
a. Build and maintain body tissues.
b. Carry iron and oxygen in the blood.
c. Form hormones, enzymes, and antibodies.
d. Provide energy.

15. Which of the following combinations demonstrates two incomplete proteins forming a complete protein?
a. Oatmeal and milk. **c.** Rice and beans.
b. Orange juice and yogurt. **d.** Steak and milk.

16. What will eventually happen if a vitamin is missing from the diet?
a. A craving for rich food sources of the vitamin will develop.
b. Deficiency symptoms will appear.
c. The body will adapt to getting along without the vitamin.
d. The body will produce the missing vitamin.

17. Which of the following is not a water-soluble vitamin?
a. Riboflavin. **c.** Vitamin B_6.
b. Vitamin A. **d.** Vitamin C.

18. What is the main function of Vitamin K?
a. Assists in the formation of muscle.
b. Helps form healthy eyes.
c. Helps the blood coagulate or clot.
d. Carries oxygen in the blood.

19. Women of childbearing age should ensure that they have enough of this nutrient in order to prevent nervous system and brain problems.
a. Thiamine.
b. Vitamin C.
c. Vitamin D.
d. Folate.

20. Which of the following is a good source of vitamin C?
a. Enriched breads and cereals.
b. Fortified margarine.
c. Grapefruit, limes, orange, lemons.
d. Milk.

21. Which of the following is a macro-mineral?
a. Calcium.
b. Selenium.
c. Folate.
d. Vitamin C.

22. Which of the following is a source of iron that is absorbed well in the body?
a. Broccoli.
b. Rice.
c. Beans.
d. Steak.

23. Which mineral is added to salt to prevent goitre?
a. Chlorine.
b. Iodine.
c. Sodium.
d. Vitamin C

24. A positive test for simple sugars would be:
a. Iodine turns purple.
b. Iodine solution stays orange.
c. Benedict's solution turns orange.
d. Benedict's solution turns purple.

25. What would test highest for starch?
a. Milk.
b. Potato chip.
c. Apple or apple juice.
d. Salad dressing.

26. What would show a positive test when mixed with Benedict's solution?
a. Rice.
b. Potato chip.
c. Apple juice.
d. Salad dressing.

27. The standard nutrient terminology that is beginning to be used by both Canada and the United States is:
a. *Canada's Food Guide to Healthy Eating*.
b. Food Guide Pyramid.
c. Dietary Reference Intake.
d. None of the above.

28. The maximum level beforewhich a nutrient may cause harm to most people is known as:
a. Recommended Dietary Allowance. **c.** Dietary Reference Intake.
b. Upper Tolerable Intake Level. **d.** All of the above.

29. According to *Canada's Food Guide to Healthy Eating*, a person should have ______ servings of grain per day.
a. 5–12. **c.** 3–4.
b. 5–10. **d.** 2–3.

30. *Canada's Food Guide to Healthy Eating* applies to people over the age of:
a. 2. **c.** 10.
b. 4. **d.** 16.

31. What factor increases BMR?
a. Lifting weights. **c.** Intake of B vitamins.
b. Personality. **d.** Your food preferences.

32. What is the safest BMI for most people?
a. Under 20. **c.** 25–27.
b. 20–25. **d.** 27 and over.

33. Energy used varies according to:
a. Muscle mass. **c.** BMR.
b. Body size. **d.** All of the above.

34. For most people, the greatest amount of energy output is from:
a. Physical activity. **c.** Basal metabolism.
b. Peristalsis. **d.** None of the above.

35. The BMI is appropriate for:
a. Pregnant women. **c.** Athletes in training.
b. Adults in their mid 20s. **d.** Growing children.

36. This is the amount of energy required to support the operation of all internal body systems:
a. BMI. **c.** BMR.
b. Peristalsis. **d.** Portal vein.

37. This range of BMI is associated with high blood pressure, heart problems, depression, and anemia:
a. Below 20 **c.** 25–27.
b. 20–25. **d.** 27 and above.

38. The BMI is calculated by:
a. Comparing waist and height measurements.
b. Comparing weight and height measurements.
c. Using insurance tables.
d. All of the above.

Part B—Thinking and Inquiry

39. The following headlines or advertisements represent common myths about the effects of nutrients in the diet. Write a rebuttal debunking the myth using the information learned in this unit. You should use terminology you have learned, including conversations, videos, notes, chapters, and worksheets.

a. "Starchy foods pack on the pounds."
b. "Bulk up on protein drinks and bulk up your muscles."
c. "A+ Vitamin and Mineral Supplements … meet your needs the easy way."
d. "Super-jolt … the pop that gives you a jolt of energy … high in sugar and caffeine."
e. "Fake fat chips … the fat will go right through you, not right on you."

Part C—Communication

40. Develop a pamphlet or poster using the slogan *"Build a Better Body from the Inside Out."* Use information from this unit to emphasize the importance of good nutrition to the public. Communicate with pictures, graphics, and symbols. Other elements to include:

- Use some wording to clarify and explain your message.
- Continue your message by using a slogan.
- Choose to focus on a specific target group (children, teenagers, parents, adults, fitness club members, people at the grocery store, health unit employees).

Note: If you find that you cannot convey all required information well in a pamphlet or poster, provide the basics in the pamphlet or poster accompanied by an information sheet describing what you have done.

Part D—Application

41. You are a nutrition researcher working in a developing country (you may choose the country). You are to develop a proposal to improve the nutrition of people in that country. You have heard of valuable research that may help others in other developing countries. Use this information to sell your proposal to the Canadian International Development Agency, which provides funding to such causes if it deems them worthy.

You may consider the following in writing your proposal:

- The chemical make-up and needs of the body (the need for different nutrients).
- Nutrition deficiency diseases (history, treatment in the past, recent initiatives, toxicities, fortification of common foods, etc.).
- *Canada's Food Guide to Healthy Eating* and other country and culture variations.
- Others.

Energy Input and Energy Output— Analysing Your Food Intake and Activity

Specific Expectations

- Compile a body of core information on the nutritional status of Canadians, using a variety of print and electronic sources and telecommunications tools (e.g., *Canada's Food Guide to Healthy Eating* and Health Canada's *Nutrition Recommendations*, computer courseware, and web sites). Determine personal nutrient intake.
- Identify the source of nutrients and the role they play in the maintenance of good health.
- Identify the role of fibre and water in the body, and the sources and roles of the major components of nutrients (e.g., carbohydrates, fats, proteins, vitamins, minerals).
- Demonstrate an understanding of the nutrients provided by foods in each category of Canada's *Food Guide to Healthy Eating* and other dietary guides and standards and, using this knowledge, describe ways to achieve healthy body weight and body image.
- Report information gathered from an existing database on the process of digestion, absorption, and metabolism of food, and on the caloric intake of individuals.
- Determine the relationship among nutrition, lifestyle, health, and disease;
- Identify the recommended daily allowances of nutrients for optimal health by gender and age.
- Communicate the results of inquiries effectively.
- Use correct terminology of food and nutrition sciences.
- Effectively communicate the results of inquiries, using a variety of methods and forms (e.g., graphs, charts, diagrams, oral presentations, written reports, and videos).

Note: You may use Student References 1–3, at the back of this manual, to assist you.

Getting Started

1. Create a three-day diary of both your activity and your food intake. Include two weekdays and one weekend day. You will hand in the diary.
2. Choose the one day that you feel is most typical of your activity and your food intake. Provide in-depth detail for both activity and food intake for your chosen day.

CULMINATING ACTIVITY—ANALYSING YOUR FOOD INTAKE AND ACTIVITY, *continued*

Analysing Your Activity

3. Make a visual presentation of your activity for the day. (You may use that day or you may use another one if you wish.)

- Show your daily activities in a visual way (pie chart, graph, chart, pictures, etc.).
- Divide the day into hourly segments. Describe the activity, the type of activity (endurance or flexibility activity, or strength training) and the calories used for each activity.
- Calculate the total calories used during the day.

Analysing Your Food Intake

4. Organize your food intake data in a chart. Provide as much detail about the food as possible (when, where, how much, etc.).

- Complete your daily nutrient intake values for one typical day. Use the "Nutrient Values of Some Common Foods" and the calculation booklet, web site with pdf file, food labels, nutrition calculation program, and/or web sites. Remember to calculate the total for the day.

5. Compare your totals to:

- *Canada's Food Guide to Healthy Eating*'s suggested servings:
  - Indicate above, below, or equal to.
  - Show your calculations for this.
  - Explain the consequences.
- *Nutrient Requirements for Adolescent Males and Females* (use Dietary Reference Intakes for Adolescents):
  - Indicate above, below, or equal to.
  - Show your calculations for this.
  - Indicate specific nutritional concerns and any associated deficiencies or toxicities that may be present.
- Make note of your water and fibre intake. Compare them to the recommendations. Comment on the functions of each of these nutrients and how you meet the standards.

Overall Analysis

6. Compare your food intake with your energy output. Indicate how your diet is meeting your daily needs and/or how you can improve your diet and/or activity level for better overall health.

Name: ______________________ Date: __________ Class: __________

Category/Expectations	Criteria	Level 1	Level 2	Level 3	Level 4
Knowledge and Understanding ■ Uses terminology associated with energy input and output. ■ Compiles a body of core information on the nutritional status of Canadians, using a variety of print and electronic sources and telecommunications tools ■ Determines personal nutrient intake.	■ Uses *Canada's Food Guide to Healthy Eating*. ■ Nutrient requirements. ■ Macronutrients (carbohydrates, proteins, and fat). ■ Micronutrients (vitamins, minerals, and water). ■ Types of exercise. ■ BMR. ■ BMI. ■ Indicators of healthy weight.				
Thinking and Inquiry ■ Identifies roles and sources of nutrients with special recognition of water and fibre. ■ Uses analysis to describe ways to achieve healthy body weight and body image. ■ Identifies the recommended daily allowances of nutrients for optimal health, by gender and age.	■ Provides comparison to personal intake. ■ Explains consequences of (specific) deficiencies. ■ Lists consequences of (specific) toxicities. ■ Recognizes water and fibre as essential to health. ■ Recognizes healthy weight. ■ Recognizes importance of active lifestyle. ■ Suggests personal improvements for a healthy, active lifestyle for optimal health.				
Communication ■ Communicates results of inquiries effectively. ■ Visuals are used in the presentation.	■ Uses visuals in the presentation: ◦ Graphs. ◦ Charts. ◦ Pictures. ■ Uses organized and meaningful format. ■ Uses correct spelling, grammar, and flow of written responses.				
Application ■ Determines personal nutrient intake, using a variety of print and electronic sources and telecommunications tools.	■ Uses tools to determine personal energy input and output. ■ Compares personal analysis of energy input and output to nutrient recommendations.				

Name: ______________________ Date: __________ Class: __________

Unit 2: Nutrition throughout the Life Cycle

2-1

What You Need to Know	Where to Find It
■ The factors that determine why people eat the foods they do.	■ Ch. 2: Why People Eat the Foods they Do (pp. 11–23) ■ Ch. 4: Food Marketing (pp. 41–51) ■ Ch. 17: Changing Perceptions of Beauty—Interacting with People (pp. 348–354)
■ The stages of the life cycle and the nutritional needs characteristic of each stage.	■ Ch. 11: Nutrient Wise—Good Nutrition and the Life Cycle (pp. 254–61) ■ Ch. 3: The Effects of Childhood Eating Patterns—Factors Influencing Children's Eating Habits (pp. 29–31) ■ Ch. 13: Personal Eating Habits (pp. 285–295)
■ Nutritional concerns and challenges faced by people in each stage in the life cycle.	■ Ch. 14: Diet, Lifestyle, and Health—Managing Health Conditions (pp. 304–313) ■ Ch. 3: The Effect of Childhood Eating Patterns—The Importance of Eating Healthy During Childhood (pp. 27–28); Childhood Obesity (pp. 32–37) ■ Ch. 9: Meal Planning and Management—Meal Planning Challenges (pp. 157–163)
■ Food Lab.	■ Baby Food Taste Testing ■ Food and the Life Cycle
■ Examples of entrepreneurship and careers associated with food and nutrition sciences.	■ Career Profiles throughout the text.
■ The different types of vegetarian regimes and reasons for being vegetarian.	■ Ch. 14: Diet, Lifestyle, and Health—The Vegetarian Lifestyles (pp. 299–304) ■ Ch. 11: Nutrient Wise—Nutrients (pp. 223–248) for review
■ Food Lab.	■ Vegging Out
■ Concepts related to Social Science research. ■ How to plan, conduct, and summarize the results of an investigation into the availability of food products for various parts of the life cycle.	■ The Social Science Research Process (p. 13) Key and Supporting Issues When Developing Questions (p. 37) Primary and Secondary Research (p. 50–51) Data Collecting (p. 290) Evaluating Sources (p. 312) Recording Key Ideas from Research (p. 335) Evidence versus Opinion (p. 349) Report Writing (p. 427) Quantitative and Qualitative Research Methods (p. 508) Developing Research Skills: Using Internet Sources (p. 600) ■ Ch. 28: Nutritional Status of Canadians (pp. 581–601)
■ Unit Culminating Activity: Conducting of a study to determine the eating habits practiced at a specific stage of the life cycle.	

Name: ______________________ Date: __________ Class: __________

2-2

DIAGNOSTIC QUIZ

Unit 2: Nutrition throughout the Life Cycle

1. Energy levels for children 1–2 years old are high. Parents should:
   a. Limit the amount of food eaten.
   b. Not limit the amount of foods eaten.
   c. Limit the amount of fat in their children's diets.
   d. All of the above.

2. Suitable foods for toddlers would include:
   a. Apples.
   b. Hotdogs.
   c. Popcorn.
   d. Cheese and crackers.

3. Colostrum is:
   a. A yellow fluid found in breast milk the first three days after birth, which helps to prevent infection.
   b. A protein powder found in feeding formulas.
   c. A cause of infection in newborn babies.
   d. None of the above.

4. What would be an appropriate serving of fruit for a 3-year-old child?
   a. A bunch of grapes (15–20).
   b. 45 ml apple sauce.
   c. 250 ml (1 cup) cooked vegetables.
   d. A peanut butter sandwich.

5. At what stage do humans grow most rapidly?
   a. Infancy.
   b. Young childhood.
   c. Adolescence.
   d. Older adulthood.

6. A(n) __________ vegetarian is one who eats only foods from plant sources.
   a. Vegan.
   b. Lacto-ovo vegetarian.
   c. Semi-vegetarian.
   d. All of the above.

7. Vitamin C helps in the absorption of __________________.
   a. Fat.
   b. Protein.
   c. Vitamin A.
   d. Iron.

8. Which is not a preventable risk factor for cancer?
   a. Diet.
   b. Smoking.
   c. Family history.
   d. Exposure to sun.

DIAGNOSTIC QUIZ, *continued*

9. In this type of diabetes, the body produces little or no insulin.
- **a.** Type 1.
- **b.** Type 2.
- **c.** Gestational.
- **d.** All of the above.

10. Research indicates that students who eat breakfast
- **a.** Perform similarly to those who don't eat breakfast.
- **b.** Perform better academically than those who don't eat breakfast.
- **c.** Don't perform as well as those who skip breakfast.
- **d.** None of the above.

11. Explain why solid foods should be introduced to an infant one at a time.

____

____

____

12. For each advertising technique, give a food-related example.

Technique	Food-related example
Limited information	
Positive images	
Celebrity endorsement	
Appeal to basic needs	
Scare tactics	
False claims	
Infomercials	

13. A young child drinks some milk and gets a stomachache. Her father notices that this happens whenever the child has any milk or milk products. Analyse the problem and make suggestions to the parent.

____

____

____

____

14. What is the risk in megadosing?

____

____

15. For whom are dietary supplements useful?

____

____

16. Type 2 diabetes used to be called "age-onset" diabetes: however, it now affects many young children. Why?

____

____

____

____

____

____

Name: ______________________ Date: __________ Class: __________

Why People Eat the Foods They Do

2-3

Instructions

- Use Chapter 2, Why People Eat the Foods They Do, pages 11–37 to develop a mind map showing the influencing factors.
- Then write a short essay (300 words) giving specific examples related to at least four of the factors.

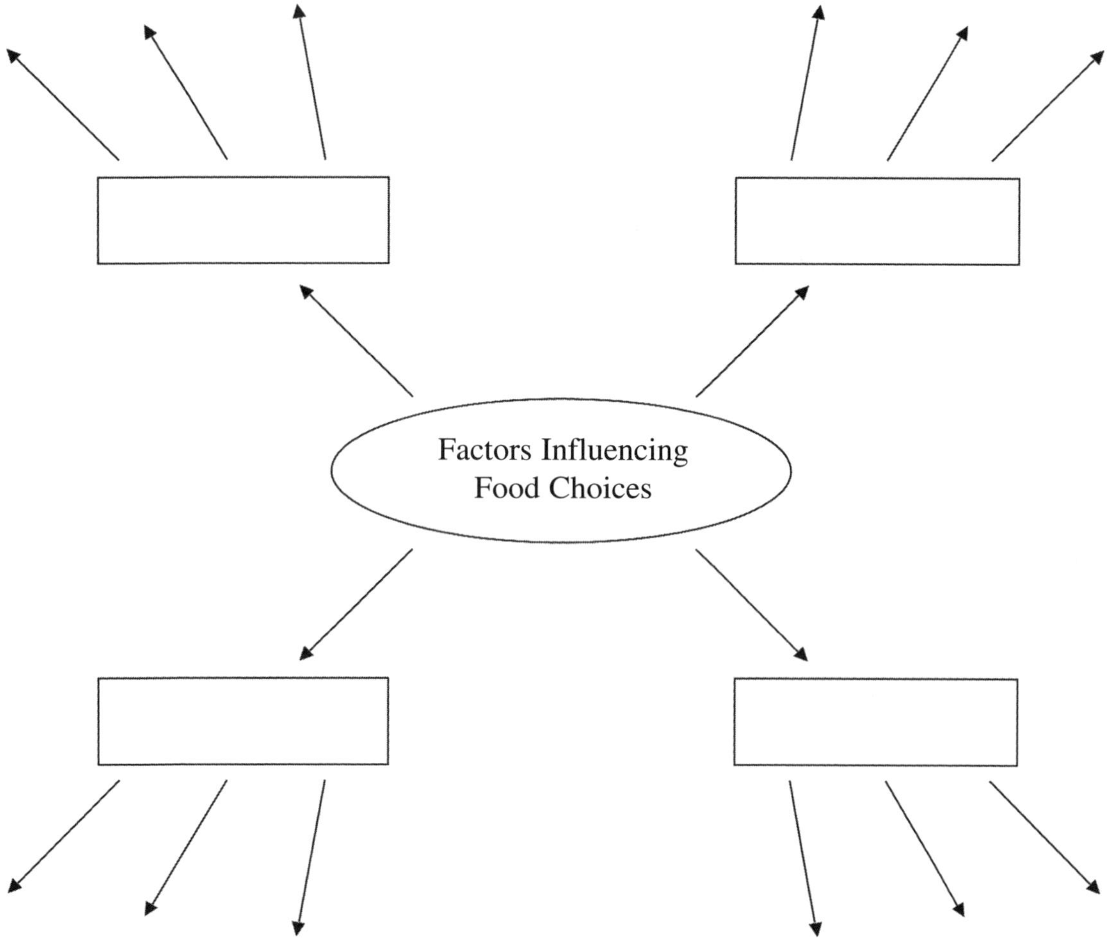

Name: ______________________ Date: __________ Class: __________

2-4

STUDY GUIDE

Food Marketing

Instructions

Read Chapter 4, Food Marketing, pages 41–51 to complete the following activity.
Answer the following questions on a separate sheet of paper:

Thinking and Inquiry

1. There are many influences affecting the foods people choose to eat including family, peers, and the media. Develop a picture timeline of your life thus far to show the main influences on what you eat. Give specific examples for three stages in your life.

2. Choose three of the statistical findings on page 43–44. Compare your typical day and your use of the media to the statistical findings. Analyse how you are influenced in your eating habits by the media you use.

Communication

3. The FYI on page 44, "Marketing to Children" notes that advertisers see children as future lifetime customers and want to make them loyal to their products at a young age. Discuss how you spend money on food. Compare what you bought as a younger child to what you buy now.

Application

4. Often several advertising techniques are used to sell a product. Think of a food advertisement. From the techniques described on pages 46–49, explain how at least three advertising techniques are used to sell the food product. You may clip a newspaper, Internet, or magazine ad and/or describe a television or radio commercial.

Name: ______________________ Date: __________ Class: __________

Eating Habits and the Life Cycle

2-5

Instructions

- For each part of the life cycle, fill in the chart.
- Consider what is commonly done at each stage, e.g., what they can do physically, what their responsibilities are, who makes their choices for them, what a typical day involves. Then on the opposite side, consider how each of the items you've listed may influence eating choices and habits.

Infants/Babies	
Characteristics of Stage	**Effects on Eating Choices and Habits**

↓

Toddlers	
Characteristics of Stage	**Effects on Eating Choices and Habits**

↓

School Age (Grades K-8)	
Characteristics of Stage	**Effects on Eating Choices and Habits**

↓

Teenagers/High School	
Characteristics of Stage	**Effects on Eating Choices and Habits**

Name: ______________________ Date: ____________ Class: ____________

2-5

EATING HABITS AND THE LIFE CYCLE, *continued*

Young Adulthood	
Characteristics of Stage	**Effects on Eating Choices and Habits**

Middle Adulthood	
Characteristics of Stage	**Effects on Eating Choices and Habits**

Pregnant and Breast-feeding Women	
Characteristics of Stage	**Effects on Eating Choices and Habits**

Older Adulthood	
Characteristics of Stage	**Effects on Eating Choices and Habits**

Name: ____________________ Date: __________ Class: __________

CAREERS IN FOOD SCIENCES AND NUTRITION

2-6

A Career for the Life Cycle

Specific Expectations

- Identify the social, psychological, economic, emotional, cultural, religious, and physical factors that affect food choices.
- Summarize food-related issues that arise throughout the life cycle.
- Determine the relationship among nutrition, lifestyle, health, and disease.
- Identify examples of entrepreneurship in the food industry, and occupations related to food and nutrition sciences.
  - Use a variety of print and electronic sources to find information on employment opportunities in areas relating to food and nutrition sciences, such as health and medicine, hospitality services, agriculture, and food technology and production.
- Use appropriate Social Science research methods in the investigation of food-related issues.
- Correctly use terminology associated with food and nutrition.
- Communicate the results of your inquiries effectively.

Your Job

There are many jobs and careers linked to food and nutritional sciences including the food industry, health care, counselling, hospitality, agriculture, food production, and so on. Many of these jobs meet the needs of or address one or more stages of the life cycle.

You are to identify a career in the food and nutrition sciences–linked field.

- Describe what this job/career typically involves:
  - Daily tasks.
  - People and/or things worked with.
  - Situations dealt with.
- Education required:
  - Education and/or training required – schools (colleges, universities, training schools) in the province and Canada that offer the program and/or similar programs.
  - Time and commitment generally required to educate and train.
  - Any additional qualifications or certifications suggested or required.
  - Skills beneficial to the role.
- Link the job to the life cycle (at least one stage)
  - Connection to the ages and stages of one or more stages of the life cycle
  - Illustrate how this is a food and nutrition sciences–related job/career (Note: the job does not have to be directly linked to food and nutrition sciences as long as you can ultimately make a connection to the stage.)
  - Describe what needs are addressed by this career.
  - How does the job affect eating habits/choices and/or the health and well-being of individuals?

Name: ______________________ Date: ____________ Class: ____________

2-6 A CAREER FOR THE LIFE CYCLE, *continued*

Your teacher may ask you to submit a written report (or a creative account) and/or address a presentation to the class or a small group.

A Career for the Life Cycle—Assessment and Evaluation

Category/ Expectations	Criteria	Level 1	Level 2	Level 3	Level 4
Knowledge and Understanding ■ Uses terminology associated with food and nutrition ■ Summarizes food-related issues that arise throughout the life cycle.	■ Related to age/stages of life cycle. ° Nutritional and food needs. ° Possible challenges or conditions.				
Thinking and Inquiry ■ Identifies the social, psychological, economic, emotional, cultural, religious, and physical factors that affect food choices. ■ Uses a variety of print and electronic sources to find information on employment opportunities in areas relating to food and nutrition sciences, such as health and medicine, hospitality services, agriculture, and food technology and production.	■ How people in each stage get their food. ° Who helps. ° Factors affecting how people in each stage get the food. ■ Careers: ° Training/education. ° Provincial and Canadian training facilities. ° Additional qualifications and/or certifications. ° Skills needed. ° Daily situations. ° People worked with.				
Communication ■ Communicates results of his or her inquiries effectively	■ Visuals are used in the presentation: ° Graphs, Charts, Pictures. ■ Organized and meaningful format. ■ Correct spelling, grammar, and flow of written responses.				
Application ■ Determines the relationship among nutrition, lifestyle, health, and disease.	■ Relationship to life cycle. ■ Relationship to food and nutrition sciences.				

Name: ______________________ Date: __________ Class: __________

2003 Report on Healthy Eating Challenges Facing Women

2-7

The National Nutrition Month Campaign in March 2003 focused on helping women find solutions to their healthy eating challenges—for both themselves and their families.

Women have unique nutritional needs throughout the different stages of their lives and still hold most of the responsibility for their family's nutrition and well-being. Typically, women make the decisions about what and how their family eats, as well as doing most of the grocery shopping and meal preparation.

The Nutrition Month campaign raises and addresses key food and nutrition challenges affecting women. Although dietitians have daily contact with women through their practices and can offer advice and practical tips on achieving healthy eating, Kraft Canada, Dairy Farmers of Canada, and Dietitians of Canada believed it was important to connect directly with women and listen to what they had to say about their own healthy eating challenges.

In August, 2002, a "Healthy Eating for Women" survey was posted on the Dietitians of Canada web site to find out more about women's nutrition concerns as well as their healthy eating challenges and solutions. The survey collected results from 174 English-speaking women and 30 French-speaking women.

A survey was also posted for dietitians to gather input on what they, as health professionals, perceived to be the food and nutrition challenges of women and what solutions they offer. This survey received results from 468 English-speaking dietitians and 25 French-speaking dietitians.

The results in this report reflect three key emerging themes: concerns regarding lack of food preparation time, difficulties in determining healthy food choices, and the role of food in achieving a healthy weight.

Survey Participants

English speaking
- 90% were women aged 24–45
- 71% lived with a spouse or partner
- 36% had at least one child under the age of 12
- 20% had at least one child 12–18 years of age
- 67% worked full time
- 80% had completed a college/university degree

French speaking
- 76% were women aged 24–45
- 70% lived with a spouse or partner
- 30% had at least one child under the age of 12
- 9% had at least one child 12–18 years of age
- 73% worked full time
- 73% had completed a college/university degree

Time ... Time ... Time ...

The biggest challenge facing women who want to eat well is time. Women reported they don't have time to plan, purchase, and prepare healthy meals and food choices. Preparing meals that the whole family likes and will eat was said to be especially hard when women are tired after a long day at work.

One survey respondent sums up the situation with, "I think my biggest challenge is trying to prepare healthy meals that are interesting for my kids and that are fast to prepare, as I work full time and am starving when I get home from work at 4:30 p.m." Yet most consumers (91%) Anglophone and 77% Francophone) agree that eating together as a family encourages healthy eating habits.

When dietitians were asked about the issues facing their female clients, a lack of time to plan and prepare meals was reported to be the biggest obstacle to eating well. They indicated that women want to eat well and maintain a healthy weight but they have difficulty achieving this while satisfying competing wants and needs of their family.

Other factors reported by dietitians that contribute to unhealthy eating habits are the gradual erosion of cooking and meal planning skills of younger women and the perceived high cost of eating well.

Healthy Food Choices

When women were asked which nutrients or ingredients they were most concerned about, fat, calories/energy, fibre, and calcium topped the list.

Dietitians report that they are most often asked about how to incorporate enough fruit, vegetables, and calcium into a regular eating routine.

When women were asked what food groups they feel are the most challenging when they want to eat well, the results varied between English and French speakers. Anglophones were more concerned with vegetables, fruit, and grain products, while Francophone women tended to raise milk products and meat as additional challenges.

Healthy Weight and Women

When asked what strategies would help the most in maintaining or achieving a healthy weight, the most common response was increasing their level of physical activity.

Eating balanced meals and controlling calorie/energy intake were the next two important strategies mentioned by English-speaking respondents. Francophone women responded slightly differently, indicating that eating healthy meals and controlling fat intake were important.

Dietitians ranked increased level of physical activity, controlling calorie/energy intake, and fat intake as the most important strategies to achieving and sustaining a healthy weight.

What Women Want

English-Speaking Consumers	French-Speaking Consumers
■ 41% More time to cook	■ 40% Tips for maintaining or achieving a healthy weight
■ 34% Menus/recipes	■ 33% More time to cook
■ 34% Simple tools to assess my food choices/eating habits	■ 34% Simple tools to assess my food choices/eating habits
■ 32% Healthy meals that taste good	■ 33% Healthy meals being available in fast-food outlets

Healthy Weight Solutions Suggested by Dietitians

1. Eat everything in moderation and avoid dieting. Instead, choose to change your overall lifestyle in the long term to improve your health.

2003 REPORT ON HEALTHY EATING CHALLENGES FACING WOMEN, *continued*

2. Work regular physical activity into the day. Understand the portion sizes outlined in *Canada's Food Guide to Healthy Eating*. Don't skip meals.
3. Don't try to do the whole healthy eating thing all at once—take small, realistic steps; work on each small change for a long time (2-4 weeks) to build it as a habit before trying something new; get more active in little ways throughout the day.

Time-Saving Tips for Healthy Meals Suggested by Canadian Women and Dietitians

1. Take the time to feed yourself, and be a healthy role model for your children to ensure they are well-nourished.
2. Enjoy eating well and trying new recipes and foods, again as a role model and to introduce your family to new, nutritious foods.
3. Cook one meal that the whole family can share. Time is essential and cooking two meals is expensive and time consuming.
4. Try brown beans and cheese rolled in a tortilla, or scrambled eggs, toast, an orange, and milk for supper. Healthy eating can be done without a recipe and in a limited amount of time.
5. Have a grocery list divided into categories—grain products, vegetables and fruit, milk products, meats and alternatives—this not only helps you to see how your food choices balance out, but it also saves time as most of the foods are located together in the store.
6. Prepare meals in advance or partial preparation the night before to shorten prep time after work.
7. Buy salad/veggies that are ready to use, or use frozen. Plan the menu and the shopping list and shop once.

Answer the following questions on a separate sheet of paper

1. Each year March is Nutrition Month. For 2003, the theme was women and healthy eating challen ges. Why were adult women the focus?

2. Compare the information regarding English- and French-speaking women. What are the most obvious similarities and differences? (see sidebar section), and how might that be significant to the study?

3. Survey information:
   a. What two different survey samples were completed and why?
   b. Describe how the researchers collected the information for the survey.
   c. Describe the advantages and disadvantages of doing a survey this way (to the researchers, the participants, and the final results).
   d. How could the survey distribution be improved?

2003 REPORT ON HEALTHY EATING CHALLENGES FACING WOMEN, *continued*

4. What three main topics or themes emerged from the research (surveys)? Describe these and give the results of each of the sample groups. Use the following chart format for each section.

Women	Dietitians

5. Create a graph to show "What women want in terms of nutrition." Include a title detailing what the graph is about, label the axes, and describe the main findings.

6. Make a chart about the three official sponsors of the research and the Dietitians of Canada. On the chart describe:

- Their reputations.
- Why the sponsors funded the research.
- Benefits to women who follow ideas and suggestions made.
- Other things sponsors are involved in

7. How does this type of information compare to other information you have learned so far in the course?

Name: ______________________ Date: __________ Class: __________

STUDY GUIDE **2-8**

Good Nutrition and the Life Cycle

Instructions

Use pages 254-261 to answer the following questions.

Knowledge and Understanding

1. Explain the following terms:

Life cycle	
Midwife	
Colostrum	

2. Why should a woman be concerned about nutrition even before she knows she is pregnant?

____

____

3. Teen pregnancy poses high risks. Why and to whom?

____

____

4. What nutrients should be stressed specifically during pregnancy?

Nutrient	Sources

5. How much weight should women gain during pregnancy?

____

Infancy

6. Breast milk is usually considered better than baby formula. Why?
   a. ____
   b. ____

7. What is formula typically made of?

____

____

8. List three suggestions for how to introduce solid foods to infants.
   a. ____
   b. ____
   c. ____

9. Suggest three healthy finger foods for infants.
   a. ____
   b. ____
   c. ____

Young Children

10. What do professionals suggest as serving sizes for young children?

____

____

11. Why are multiple meals each day recommended for young children?

____

____

12. List four suggestions for fostering good eating habits in young children.

a. ______________________

b. ______________________

c. ______________________

d. ______________________

Adolescence

13. Why are teens often hungry and snack frequently?

____

____

Adulthood

14. List three problems associated with the eating habits of older adults.

a. ______________________

____

b. ______________________

____

c. ______________________

____

Name: ______________________ Date: __________ Class: __________

2-9

FOOD LAB

Taste Testing Baby Food

Instructions

Your teacher will provide you with a selection of unlabelled or unmarked baby foods. You are to taste test several of the foods and examine their texture. Try to identify the selections.

Product #	Appearance	Texture	Flavour(s) Description	What Is It?
1.				
2.				
3.				
4.				
5.				
6.				
7.				
8.				
9.				

Questions

Thinking and Inquiry

1. What are some common characteristics of baby food?

EXPERIMENT—TASTE TESTING BABY FOOD, *continued*

2. Why are the flavours somewhat milder than adult food?

3. What other foods are provided to babies at this time?

4. There is also toddler food available in jars. How might this food differ from baby food?

5. Examine the food labels for both the ingredients and the nutrition information/facts. What ingredients are commonly present and which are not?

6. If you were preparing a meal for your family and a baby, what would you do to make the food suitable for the baby?

Name: ______________________ Date: __________ Class: __________

2-10

STUDY GUIDE

The Effects of Childhood Eating Patterns

Instructions

Use pages 27–37 to answer the following questions.

Knowledge and Understanding

1. There are different types of eating disorders. List and describe three.

2. Why are childhood eating patterns so important?

3. Describe how obesity influences the following conditions:

Condition	How Obesity Influences It
Self-esteem	
Breathing disorders	
Bone and joint problems	
Diabetes	
High cholesterol	
Gall bladder disease	
High blood pressure and hypertension	
Stroke	
Heart disease	

STUDY GUIDE—THE EFFECTS OF CHILDHOOD EATING PATTERNS, *continued*

Thinking and Inquiry

4. How might parents send mixed messages about food?

5. Why should parents be cautious about using food as a reward or punishment?

6. List four rules or guidelines to help children build healthy eating habits.
   a. ______________________
   b. ______________________
   c. ______________________
   d. ______________________

7. What are the contributing factors to obesity in children?
   a. ______________________
   b. ______________________
   c. ______________________
   d. ______________________

8. How do statistics about weight compare between 1981 and 1991?

9. What is the association between watching television and obesity?

Name: ________________ Date: ________ Class: ________

2-11

ISSUE

"Teen girls get less nutrients than boys"

The Canadian Press
October 25, 2000

TORONTO—Teen girls are more likely than teen boys to skimp on certain important foods, suggests a nutrition study released Tuesday.

Researchers at Montreal's McGill University studied 177 young people aged 13 to 17 and found the girls and boys were getting "reasonable" amounts of fat in their diets.

But the girls in the study didn't eat as much milk, milk products, meats and other high-protein foods as the boys, said Katherine Gray-Donald of McGill's school of dietetics and human nutrition.

As a result, the girls' diets tended to be low in calcium and borderline in iron and zinc.

"I expect concerns about fat and body size are at least one reason why girls are not eating enough meat and dairy products," said Gray-Donald.

On average, fat contributed 31 per cent of energy for the boys in the study and 27 per cent for girls, which is in line with suggested daily intakes.

But there's concern that teens are getting the wrong fats, from fast foods such as french fries and chocolate bars which have little nutritional value.

"We know that teens like to snack and eat with their friends," said Gray-Donald.

"We need to help teens to select appropriate meals when eating out. That could be as simple as enjoying popular choices such as hamburgers, cheeseburgers, submarine sandwiches, pizza, tacos and wraps with milk or low-fat milkshakes, real juices, salads and fruit."

McGill's research team presented its findings at a recent conference in Ottawa of the Canadian Public Health Association. The look into teen eating habits is part of a larger study released last year involving 1,700 teens and adults which indicated Canadians appear to be cutting back on their fat consumption and are generally eating better.

The study was funded by the Beef Industry Development Fund which involves the beef industry.

(**Source**: http://www.canoe.ca/Health0010/25_nutrition-cp.html. Retrieved May 12, 2004.)

Questions

Thinking and Inquiry

1. Comment on the reliability or validity of this study.

2. Describe the sample group.

3. What do you think the initial research was trying to determine? (What was the research question?)

4. What was the main finding? What do the findings suggest?

Findings	Possible Suggestions for Findings

5. How does the intake of fat compare with that suggested by experts?

6. What is the significance of the funding for the study?

Name: ____________________ Date: __________ Class: __________

2-12

STUDY GUIDE

Managing Health Concerns

Instructions

Use pages 304–311 to answer the following questions.

Knowledge and Understanding

1. Define the following terms:

Dietary supplements	
Megadose	
Homocysteine	
Diabetes	
Insulin	
Cancer	
Food allergy	
Food intolerance	

2. List three ways to help care for someone who is ill or recovering from an illness.

a. ____________________

b. ____________________

c. ____________________

3. For whom may supplements be useful?

4. What do critics say about megadosing?

5. What do natural health products include?

6. List four roles of the *Office of Natural Health Products.*

   a. ______________________________

   b. ______________________________

   c. ______________________________

   d. ______________________________

Special Eating Plans

7. Fill in the blanks on the chart below.

Condition	Prevention(s)	Nutrients and/or Foods for Special Consideration
High cholesterol		
High blood pressure		
Homocysteine and heart disease	Reducing levels of homocysteine by taking in foods high in certain nutrients	
Diabetes		High fibre foods Well-balanced diet
HIV/AIDS		
Osteoporosis	Limit salt intake Weight-bearing exercise Foods rich in calcium, vitamin D, and phosphorus	
Cancer		Rich, dark-green leafy vegetables; fruits
Food allergy		Common foods that people may be allergic to include peanuts, cow's milk, eggs, wheat, and soy
Food intolerance	For example, intolerance to milk may cause digestive problems	

Name: ______________________ Date: __________ Class: __________

8. Differentiate between the types of diabetes.

Type 1	
Type 2	
Gestational	

9. List four other health problems associated with diabetes.

a. ______________________

b. ______________________

c. ______________________

d. ______________________

10. List four known risk factors for cancer.

a. ______________________

b. ______________________

c. ______________________

d. ______________________

11. What types of allergic reactions to food may people have?

Name: ______________________ Date: __________ Class: __________

2-13 **FOOD LAB**

Foods and the Life Cycle

Specific Expectations

- Identify the factors that affect personal food choices throughout the life cycle (e.g., age, health, school and/or work schedules, lifestyle, level of physical activity, lactation, special dietary needs).
- Plan a menu for, select, and prepare foods that would meet selected dietary needs during the different stages of life.
- Identify the source of nutrients and the role they play in the maintenance of good health.
- Explain the relationship among lifestyle, food choices, and nutrition-related illnesses and diseases (e.g., cardiovascular disease, anorexia nervosa, tooth decay, osteoporosis).
- Correctly use terminology associated with food and nutrition.
- Communicate the results of their inquiries effectively.

Your Role

You are a chef on a community health team. Your team is developing an informative cookbook with recipes for people in each stage of the life cycle. Each chapter of the book addresses a specific stage. You and your lab group are responsible for producing one chapter devoted to a specific stage of the life cycle. Your teacher may choose the stage for you or you may do this by drawing from a hat.

Target Group

- Your target group is people in your specific stage of the life cycle.

About Your Chapter

- Make your chapter interesting to people in your assigned stage of the life cycle; talk to your key audience.
- Provide an introduction to catch their attention. Address the interests of the age group. Consider who is responsible for the food preparation for that group (i.e., for toddler, you are likely talking to parents, for older adults, you may talk to them and/or their loved ones, etc.)
- You are required to find or make up at least five healthy recipes to include in your chapter. Provide an introduction for each recipe describing why it is good for people in this stage of the life cycle.
- Illustrate the recipes or nutrient needs so readers will understand and remember the key concepts about their nutrient and food needs.

Preparing the Recipes

- Choose one of your recipes to plan and prepare.
  - List the equipment you will need to prepare the recipe from start to finish.
  - Give a list of ingredients needed to the teacher. Your teacher and your group will determine what is already on hand, and what must be purchased and by whom.

Foods and the Life Cycle Assessment and Evaluation

Category/Expectation	Criteria	Level 1	Level 2	Level 3	Level 4
Knowledge and Understanding ■ Identify the factors that affect personal food choices throughout the life cycle. ■ Correctly use terminology associated with food and nutrition.	■ Identifies specific target group and the factors that affect their food choices and habits. ■ Chapter uses terminology specific to the life cycle, nutrients, conditions and diseases, and eating habits.				
Thinking and Inquiry ■ Plan a menu for, select, and prepare foods that meet selected dietary needs during the different stages of life. ■ Explain the relationship among lifestyle, food choices, and nutrition-related illnesses and diseases. ■ Identify the source of nutrients and the role they play in the maintenance of good health.	■ Connects foods prepared to dietary needs during stage of life cycle. ■ Identifies common conditions, diseases, or challenges faced by the group. ■ Connects food and recipes to the nutrient needs of the group to maintain health and/or prevent common conditions or diseases.				
Communication ■ Effectively communicate the results of your inquiries, using a variety of methods and forms (e.g., graphs, charts, diagrams, oral presentations, written reports, videos).	■ Presents chapter in organized manner. ■ Directs advertisement at target group. ■ Presents introduction and added information in an interesting format.				
Application ■ Plan a menu for, select, and prepare foods that meet selected dietary needs during the different stages of life.	■ Produces recipe. ■ Provides and negotiates grocery list. ■ Provides and negotiates equipment list.				

Name: ______________________ Date: __________ Class: __________

2-14

Shopping for Life

Specific Expectations

- Identify psychological and emotional factors that affect eating habits.
- Describe the sociocultural importance of food in social interactions.
- Describe economic factors that have an impact on the food choices of individuals and families.
- Identify the factors that affect personal food choices.
- Identify the source of nutrients and the role they play in the maintenance of good health;
- Explain the relationship among lifestyle, food choices, and nutrition-related illnesses and diseases.
- Correctly use terminology associated with food and nutrition.
- Communicate the results of your inquiries effectively.

Grocery stores are full of food products and advertising directed at people in different stages of the life cycle. For example, the cereal aisle stocks a large number of cereals, often high in sugar and relatively low in nutrients, marketed directly to children who want them for the prizes, cartoon characteristics, and sweet flavours.

You were hired by the grocery store to determine whether it is meeting the needs of people in all stages of the life cycle. After investigating the food products available in the store, you will report to the store on what it is doing well, and what it could/should do to improve.

Your Job

- You are to pick a specific stage of the life cycle and examine the relevant food products and information available in your local grocery store.
- Describe the factors that influence why each group eats the foods it does. You should speak about the group in general, and then be specific about the facilities and resources available in your own community.
- The following should be taken into consideration when identifying the food products available. Note that many products will not be specifically marketed to certain age groups. It is your job to connect food products and stages in the life cycle.

  Consider:
  - Why a group typically may not eat well.
  - What nutrients are needed specifically for the group.
  - Health problems of people in the group who do not eat properly (quantity and quality of food).
  - Why these nutrients are needed

Name: ______________________ Date: __________ Class: __________

Shopping for Life
Assessment and Evaluation

Category/Expectations	Criteria	Level 1	Level 2	Level 3	Level 4
Knowledge and Understanding ■ Correctly use terminology associated with food and nutrition.	For the stage selected, identifies: ■ Nutritional and food needs. ■ Possible challenges or conditions.				
Thinking and Inquiry ■ Identify the source of nutrients and the role they play in the maintenance of good health. ■ Identify the factors that affect personal food choices.	■ Connects to the life cycle stage: ° Nutritionally ° Socially ° Psychologically ° Physically ° Economically ° Within the family ■ Connects to special needs, conditions and/or diseases				
Communication ■ Communicate the results of your inquiries effectively.	Communicates to the specific target group in the life cycle stage. ■ Organizes the products found according to the evidence ■ Uses proper spelling and grammar.				
Application ■ Explain the relationship among lifestyle, food choices, and nutrition-related illnesses and diseases.	■ Provides suggestions to grocery store as to what it is doing well. ■ Makes suggestions for improvement.				

Name: ______________________ Date: __________ Class: __________

2-15

STUDY GUIDE

Vegetarian Lifestyles

Instructions

Use pages 299-304 to answer the following questions.

Knowledge and Understanding

1. There are several kinds of vegetarians. List and describe the variations.

Vegan	
Lacto vegetarian	
Ovo vegetarian	
Lacto-ovo vegetarian	
Semi-vegetarian	

2. List three religions that tend to be vegetarian as part of their beliefs.

   a. ______________________

   b. ______________________

   c. ______________________

3. What foods are included in the "alternatives" of meat and alternatives?

4. Since plants do not contain all the essential amino acids, how does an individual get all they need?

VEGETARIAN LIFESTYLES, *continued*

5. Which vegetarian foods are high in fats?

6. What is the function of iron in the body?

7. How can the absorption of plant protein be improved?

8. List three ways vegetarians can be sure to get enough calcium in their diets.
   a. ______________________
   b. ______________________
   c. ______________________

9. List four groups of people who are most likely to be missing important nutrients if they are vegetarians.
   a. ______________________
   b. ______________________
   c. ______________________
   d. ______________________

Name: ______________________ Date: __________ Class: __________

2-16

FOOD LAB

Vegging Out

Specific Expectations

- Identify the social, psychological, economic, emotional, cultural, religious, and physical factors that affect food choices.
- Summarize food-related issues that arise throughout the life cycle (vegetarianism).
- Identify the source of nutrients and the role they play in the maintenance of good health.
- Determine the relationship among nutrition, lifestyle, health, and disease.
- Describe the types of vegetarian dietary regimens and the reasons people adopt them
- Use available resources, including computer technology, both to plan a menu consisting of foods that will maintain good health, and to select and prepare those foods.
- Use appropriate Social Science research methods in the investigation of food-related issues.
- Correctly use the terminology of food and nutrition sciences.
- Summarize and interpret articles on food and nutrition found in newspapers, magazines, and selected research literature, as well as on the internet.
- Effectively communicate the results of their inquiries.

Your Role

You are a community health adviser working with teenagers who are considering becoming or have recently become vegetarians. You are aware that teens may be or become vegetarians for a variety of reasons. Many do not take in enough nutrients to maintain good health.

Target Group

Your target group is teenagers. They have signed up for an after-school workshop to learn more about being healthy vegetarians.

Your Workshop

- Provide an introduction to the teenagers. Discuss why people become vegetarian.
- Describe the advantages and disadvantages of a vegetarian diet.
- Talk about the different kinds or levels of vegetarianism.

FOOD LAB—VEGGING OUT, *continued*

- Explain why people are vegetarians.
- Identify nutrients vegetarians need to be especially concerned about getting in their diets.
- Help the teenagers learn about and understand the importance of complementary proteins.
- Provide three to five recipes that would be suitable for this group.
- Provide three sources of information other than your textbook, citing them in APA style.
- Choose one of your recipes to plan and prepare. It should be a healthy and delicious representative of vegetarian recipes, and meet your group's dietary needs.
- List the equipment you will need to prepare the recipe from start to finish.
- Give the teacher a list of ingredients needed. Your teacher and your group will determine what is already on hand, what must be purchased, and by whom.

Name: ______________________ Date: __________ Class: __________

Vegging Out—Assessment and Evaluation

Category/Expectations	Criteria	Level 1	Level 2	Level 3	Level 4
Knowledge and Understanding ■ Describe the types of vegetarian dietary regimens and the reasons people adopt them ■ Correctly use the terminology of food and nutrition sciences.	■ Addresses specific target group and the factors that affect their food choices and habits: ° Psychological ° Physical ° Cultural/religious ° Environmental ° Economical ■ Workshop uses terminology specific to vegetarianism, including: ° Nutrients ° Conditions and diseases ° Complementary proteins				
Thinking and Inquiry ■ Identify the source of nutrients and the role they play in the maintenance of good health. ■ Identify the social, psychological. economic, emotional, cultural, religious and physical factors that affect food choices. ■ Determine the relationship among nutrition, lifestyle, health, and disease. ■ Summarize and interpret articles on food and nutrition found in newspapers, magazines, and selected research literature, as well as on the Internet	■ Identifies nutrients most important in vegetarianism. ■ Determines advantages and disadvantages of adopting a vegetarian lifestyle. ■ Uses 3–5 resources. ■ Develops reference list using APA style.				
Communication ■ Effectively communicate the results of your inquiries, using a variety of methods and forms (e.g., graphs, charts, diagrams, oral presentations, written reports, videos).	■ Presents workshop in organized manner. ■ Language is suitable to teen audience. ■ Provides visuals to promote understanding. ■ Proper spelling and grammar.				
Application ■ Use available resources, including computer technology, both to plan a menu consisting of foods that will maintain good health, and to select and prepare those foods.	■ Prepares representative vegetarian recipe. ■ Provides and negotiates grocery list. ■ Provides and negotiates equipment list.				

Name: ______________________ Date: __________ Class: __________

2-17

Unit 2 Test Bank

1. More than half the food commercials children view on television are devoted to:
   - **a.** Milk and milk products.
   - **b.** Vegetables and fruits.
   - **c.** High-fibre bread products.
   - **d.** High calorie or fat foods.

2. Which of the following is an example of using food to deal with emotions?
   - **a.** Eating when really sad.
   - **b.** Eating lunch with friends.
   - **c.** Eating because you're hungry.
   - **d.** Eating something after seeing an ad for it on TV.

3. Denying a child a snack because he or she won't clean up the toys is an example of:
   - **a.** Monitoring a child's weight.
   - **b.** Using food as love.
   - **c.** Using food as punishment.
   - **d.** None of the above.

4. According to nutritionists a key concern with teen pregnancy is:
   - **a.** Teens with poor diets don't have the nutrient reserves to meet the needs of a developing fetus.
   - **b.** Teens are not capable of following a doctor's advice.
   - **c.** Teens are not capable of giving adequate love.
   - **d.** All of the above.

5. The major concern about using alcohol during pregnancy is:
   - **a.** It increases morning sickness.
   - **b.** It decreases the mother's appetite.
   - **c.** It is passed directly to the baby through the placenta and may alter growth and/or lead to FAS.
   - **d.** There is no real concern.

6. A pregnant woman (or one trying to get pregnant) should be advised to increase the amount of ______________________ in her diet.
   - **a.** Vitamins and minerals (with special emphasis on folates).
   - **b.** Fat.
   - **c.** Caffeine.
   - **d.** All of the above.

7. For infants, what is usually offered as the first solid food?
   - **a.** Pureed vegetables and fruits, and even pureed meats.
   - **b.** Infant cereals.
   - **c.** Fresh fruit.
   - **d.** Pizza.

8. Why is it recommended that new foods be introduced to small children slowly, one at a time?
   - **a.** To identify allergies.
   - **b.** To avoid confusing the baby.
   - **c.** To keep the baby's weight stable.
   - **d.** So that if the baby spits up, it won't be as messy.

9. A day care provider is planning a snack for the toddler class. Which food(s) will meet the developing needs of a growing 3-year-old?
   - **a.** Peanut butter-chocolate chip cookies and a grape drink.
   - **b.** Orange pop and popcorn.
   - **c.** Apple slices and graham crackers.
   - **d.** Milk and pepperoni.

10. Which group is mostly likely to experience cracked and/or broken bones?
    - **a.** Babies who frequently fall when learning to walk.
    - **b.** School-age kids who fall during sports and other activities.
    - **c.** Women giving birth.
    - **d.** Older adults walking up and down stairs or slipping and falling.

11. A recommended weight gain for a healthy pregnancy is __________.
    - **a.** 4.5–5.4 kg (10–12 pounds).
    - **b.** 6.8–9 kg (15–20 pounds).
    - **c.** 9–15.8 kg (20–35 pounds).
    - **d.** 18.4–27 kg (40–60 pounds).

12. Colostrum is:
    - **a.** A protein powder found in feeding formulas.
    - **b.** A yellow fluid that is rich in protein and antibodies, and found in a mother's breast milk during the first three days after childbirth.
    - **c.** Leads to infection in newborn babies.
    - **d.** All of the above.

13. A vegetarian who eats no meats of any kind, but does eat milk products and eggs is:
    - **a.** Vegan.
    - **b.** Ovo-lacto vegetarian.
    - **c.** Semi-vegetarian.
    - **d.** Pollo-pesca vegetarian.

14. Iron is better absorbed in the presence of ________________.
- **a.** Vitamin C.
- **b.** Vitamin D.
- **c.** Protein.
- **d.** Calcium.

15. This type of diabetes results when the body produces insulin, but cannot use it.
- **a.** Type 1.
- **b.** Type 2.
- **c.** Homocysteine.
- **d.** Osteoporosis.
- **e.** All of the above.

16. Which condition is associated with excess amounts of the amino acid homocysteine?
- **a.** Food allergy.
- **b.** High cholesterol.
- **c.** Diabetes.
- **d.** Heart disease.

17. Food-related advertising techniques include:
- **a.** Celebrity endorsements.
- **b.** Limited information.
- **c.** Scare tactics
- **d.** All of the above.

18. Which of the following would be considered a natural health product?
- **a.** Herbal medicines.
- **b.** Homeopathic preparations.
- **c.** Mineral supplements.
- **d.** All of the above.

19. According to research (Moscovitch, 1998), it has been found that marketers and advertisers appeal to ______________________ to make loyal customers for life.
- **a.** Infants.
- **b.** Children.
- **c.** Parents.
- **d.** Older adults.

20. Teen girls tend to be lacking in which of the following nutrients:
- **a.** Vitamin D, magnesium, and fibre.
- **b.** Calcium, iron, and zinc.
- **c.** Carbohydrates, fats, and vitamin E.
- **d.** Protein, salt, and sugar.

21. Canadian women have which of the following concerns about nutrition:
  a. Finding enough time to prepare meals.
  b. Controlling fat and calorie intake.
  c. Needing time to increase their physical activity
  d. All of the above.

Application

1. Develop a case study to show aspects and considerations regarding nutrition for a specific age group. Remember to consider relationships within the group. For example, if you are writing a case study about a baby, take into account the parents and their concerns. If you are writing about teenagers, the case study must take into consideration parents, peers, school and so on.

In developing the case study, choose a specific age group and consider:

- Special nutritional needs of the group.
- Issues for the group (social, economic, physical, psychological influences, etc.).
- Food-related diseases or problems associated with the group.
- Suggestions to help the group eat healthier.

2. Families face many stresses when trying to achieve proper nutrition and well-being for all members. Create an information fact sheet to help families deal with the challenges of good nutrition. Provide specific suggestions for meeting the challenges of each life stage.

Communication

3. Discuss the role of marketing and advertising in influencing the food choices that people make.

4. Today, many people who experience one health problem also have others, including high blood pressure, high cholesterol, heart problems, diabetes, and obesity; some may also be more prone to getting cancer. Explain possible reasons for this trend.

Name: ______________________ Date: __________ Class: __________

CULMINATING ACTIVITY **2-18**

Social Science Research

Specific Expectations

- Identify the social, psychological, economic, emotional, cultural, religious, and physical factors that affect food choices.
- Plan, perform, and present the results of an investigation into the nutritional status of Canadians.
- Describe noticeable trends in food-consumption patterns.
- Demonstrate the effective use of data-collection skills and methods, including questionnaires, interviews and surveys
- Use appropriate Social Science research methods in the investigation of food-related issues.
- Summarize and interpret articles on food and nutrition found in newspapers, magazines, and selected research literature, as well as on the Internet.
- Correctly use terminology associated with food and nutrition.
- Effectively communicate the results of your inquiries, using a variety of methods and forms.

You are highly experienced Social Science researchers in the field of food and nutrition sciences. As a result, you have been invited to the prestigious symposium entitled Food and Nutrition Sciences Research for the 21st Century and Beyond. This year's focus is research related to the eating habits of groups within the family life cycle. You have been asked to present your most recent and valuable research at this meeting.

In order to prepare for the presentation, you and your colleagues must conduct the research you will present. Here's how to get started.

Step #1 Secondary Research
■ Identify the main topic. ° The issues you are concentrating on.
■ What's already out there? ° Find at least three articles related to your topic. ° Skim over the articles to check their suitability. ° Provide proper citations for them (APA).
■ Formulate the question. ° From your initial research, formulate a more precise question that you would like to learn more about. It should be more specific about your chosen topic.

Name: ____________________ Date: __________ Class: __________

Step #2 **Primary Research**
■ Examine the key issues. ° Look at your articles more closely and come up with three subtopics for your research question. ° Consider these the answers to your research question
■ Sample group. ° Clearly identify your target group for your research.
■ Methodology (a survey). ° Develop a survey to help determine if your sample group is similar or different from those studied in existing research. ° This will allow you to compare primary and secondary research.
Step #3 **Presenting Data and Comparing to the Secondary Research**
■ Complete three graphics from information in your survey. ° Use charts, graphs, etc. ° Compare this to secondary data (your articles) or to *Food for Today, First Canadian Edition.*
■ Compare your data (primary) to secondary. ° Cross-reference the data you have presented with the articles you found (you should be able to see similarities and/or differences) ° Clearly cite the research you are comparing it to in APA style.
Step #4 **Presentation to the Delegates at the Symposium**
■ Do a formal presentation of the information described above to the symposium. Remember: ° Be well prepared. ° Be clear. ° Be organized as above. ° Include visuals. ° Involve the whole group. ° Have smooth transitions between presenters. ° Keep within a 5–10 minute period for each presentation. Note: Your teacher may require a written summary and/or a presentation.

Culminating Activity—Assessment and Evaluation, continued

Category/Expectations	Criteria	Level 1	Level 2	Level 3	Level 4
Knowledge and Understanding ■ Identify the factors that affect food choices. ■ Correctly use terminology associated with food and nutrition	■ Links topic to foods and nutrition throughout the life cycle. ■ Articles show use of key terms related to nutritional needs throughout the life cycle				
Thinking and Inquiry ■ Record information and key ideas gathered from your research, and document sources accurately, using correct forms of citation. ■ Summarize and interpret articles on food and nutrition found in newspapers, magazines, and selected research literature, as well as on the Internet. ■ Compile information from a variety of primary research sources and secondary sources.	■ Cites each article using APA style. ■ Selected articles are varied. ■ Selected articles are appropriate for the topic. ■ Develops survey. ■ Survey questions relate key ideas (subtopics) found in secondary research				
Communication ■ Effectively communicate the results of your inquiries, using a variety of methods and forms.	Survey: ■ Includes introduction. ■ Uses appropriate questions. ■ Uses proper spelling and grammar. ■ Is well organized.				

Category/Expectations	Criteria	Level 1	Level 2	Level 3	Level 4
Communication ■ Plan, perform, and present the results of an investigation into the nutritional status of Canadians.	Graphs: ■ Information is important to the research question and subtopics. ■ Are fully titled and labelled. ■ Convey data effectively. Presentation: ■ Is well organized. ■ Is interesting. ■ Uses a variety of visuals. ■ Is presented using a clear voice. ■ Is engaging.				
Application ■ Demonstrate the effective use of data-collection skills and methods, including questionnaires, interviews, and surveys. ■ Plan, perform, and present the results of an investigation into the nutritional status of Canadians. ■ Describe noticeable trends in food-consumption patterns.	■ Uses appropriate sample group for the life cycle. ■ Distributes surveys. ■ Collects surveys. ■ Develops appropriate research question. ■ Deals with subtopics. ■ Forms conclusions from the results of the survey. ■ Makes suggestions as a result of the research.				

Name: ______________________ Date: __________ Class: __________

Unit 3: Canada and the Global Food Supply

3-1

What You Need to Know	Where to Find It
■ Consider common aspects of cuisines around the world. ■ Identify the role of staple foods as the core element in any cuisine. ■ Plan and prepare foods considering limited availability of resources. ■ Investigate flavours such as herbs and spices. ■ Consider the conventions of preparing, serving, and consuming foods.	■ Ch. 30: World Cuisines (pp. 624–645) o Africa (pp. 625–628) o North Africa and Southwest Asia (pp. 628–630) o South Asia (pp. 630–634) o Europe (pp. 634–640) o Latin America (pp. 640–642) ■ Ch. 26: Staple Foods of the World (pp. 528–547) o Herbs and Spices (pp. 614–615) ■ Ch. 29: Trends in Food Preparation and Consumption in Canada
■ Foods Lab	■ Breads and So Much More
■ Determine the outcomes of over- and undernutrition and deficiency diseases.	■ Food Security and Hunger (pp. 670–685) o Micronutrient Deficiencies (pp. 673–676) o Malnutrition (pp. 677–678) o The Downward Spiral of Malnutrition (pp. 678)
■ Factors affecting food production and security	■ Ch. 25: Investigating World Hunger o The Global View of Hunger (pp. 517–522)
■ Considering Fair Trade	■ Conscientious Chocolate article
■ Organizations, agencies, and causes to combat the hunger problem	■ Ch. 25: Investigating World Hunger o Hunger (pp. 513–516) o Hunger in Rural Canada (pp. 516–517) o Research Improves Crop Yields, Farmer Income, and Nutrition (pp. 520–521) o Policy and Global Food Security (pp. 522–525) ■ Ch. 32: Food Security and Hunger o Responses to Food Insecurity (pp. 679–681) o Food Security in Canada (pp. 682–683)
■ Social Science primary research to determine resources in the community (local or global	■ Interview with a person combating hunger
■ Foods Lab	■ Making recipe given limited resources (costing it). ■ Using typical basic foods that would be available from the food bank
■ Unit Culminating Activity: A Chef's Tour—Social Science primary research to determine resources in the community (local or global)	SUPPLEMENTAL INFORMATION ■ Ch. 23: Canada's Regional Foods (pp. 476–493) ■ Ch. 24: Canadian Food Supply and Production (pp. 494–511) ■ Ch. 27: Diversity in Food (pp. 548–577)

Unit 3: Diagnostic Quiz

Multiple Choice

1. Food banks in Canada
  a. Are a major response to food insecurity in Canada.
  b. Are decreasing in number over the past years.
  c. Were first established during the Depression.
  d. All of the above.

2. Vitamin A deficiency may lead to
  a. Anemia
  b. Maternal haemorrhaging.
  c. Blindness.
  d. Cretinism.

3. This grain can easily grow in poor soil and can be stored for many years. It is used to prevent food shortages in areas where drought is common.
  a. Rice.
  b. Corn.
  c. Millet.
  d. Wheat..

4. Cilantro is a herb most common in which region of the world?
  a. North America.
  b. South and Central America.
  c. Sub-Saharan Africa.
  d. Southeast Asia.

5. In which region is it common to eat with the hands rather than with utensils?
  a. Middle East.
  b. Sub-Saharan Africa.
  c. South and Central America.
  d. All of the above

True and False

6. In some developing countries, many families use nearly all of their income to buy food.
  a. True.
  b. False.

7. Overpopulation in developing countries is a concern because of the overuse and depletion of resources throughout the world.
  a. True.
  b. False.

8. The main cause of hunger in the world is overpopulation.
  a. True.
  b. False.

9. The incidence of HIV/AIDS is growing in sub-Saharan Africa.
   a. True. **b.** False.

10. Chocolate is a staple food of many countries.
   a. True. **b.** False.

Short Answer

11. Many experts indicate that there is enough food to feed the entire world's population. Why is there so much hunger?

12. Describe, using examples, the five factors below, which influence the availability of food in different areas.

Factor	Effects on Food Security
Economics	
Fuel Shortages	
Overpopulation	
War and Politics	
Natural Disasters	

13. What programs to combat hunger are available in your community?

14. List some typical foods of the five countries listed below. Describe the ingredients and/or flavours that are favoured.

Country	Common Foods	Main Ingredients
Mexico		
Russia		
India		
Greece		
China		

Name: ______________________ Date: __________ Class: __________

STUDY GUIDE 3-3

World Cuisines

Instructions

Use Chapter 30: World Cuisines, (pp. 624–645) to answer the following questions.

1. How has globalization changed eating habits?

2. Create charts like the one below on the staples, foods, and food customs for various regions. Make additional charts for: North Africa, Southeast Asia, South Asia, Northern Europe, and Latin America.

Sub-Saharan Africa	
Countries	
Staples/Common Foods	**Customs/Cuisines** **Factors affecting the foods available**

Name: ______________________ Date: __________ Class: __________

3-4

STUDY GUIDE

Staple Foods of the World

Instructions

Use Chapter 26: Staple Foods of the World (pp. 528–547) and Herbs and Spices (pp. 614–616) in Chapter 29: Trends in Food Preparation and Consumption in Canada to complete the worksheet.

Knowledge and Understanding

1. Organize the following concepts into a "food time line".
   - Settlements in agricultural areas.
   - Dropping Seeds.
   - Farming.
   - Irrigation.
   - Domestication of animals.

2. What are the most common staple foods?

3. How does each of the factors listed below affect the growing of staple foods?

Factor	Examples of Effects
Geography	
Climate	
Rainfall	

Name: ______________________ Date: __________ Class: __________

STAPLE FOODS OF THE WORLD, *continued*

3-4

4. Fill in the following chart about staple foods.

Staple Grain	Nutritional Value	Main Producers	Foods Commonly Prepared	Other Important Information
Wheat				
Corn/Maize				
Rice				
Millet				
Potatoes				
Wheat				
Sorghum				
Bananas/ Plantain				
Cassava				
Yams				

Thinking and Inquiry

5. Staple crops in your region..
   a. Consider the geography, climate, and rainfall in your immediate region. Explain what staple crops are grown there and why.

   b. Besides staple foods, what other food products are produced in your area?

   c. What foods are typical of other regions in Canada and why? Give three examples.

6. What are the differences between herbs and spices?

Herbs	Spices

Communication

7. Describe and characterize the flavours and typical herbs and spices used in at least four different countries and/or regions of the world.

Name: ______________________ Date: __________ Class: __________

FOOD LAB **3-5**

Bread and So Much More

Specific Expectations

- Plan menus for, select, and prepare foods, taking into consideration economic, geographical, and seasonal factors that affect the availability of ingredients.
- Identify the components and foods that form the basis of various cuisines around the world.
- Identify the economic, political, and environmental factors that affect food production and supply throughout the world.
- Identify the components of a cuisine (e.g., staple foods, conventions of service and consumption, utensils).
- Describe a selection of the wide variety of tastes and food preferences displayed by societies around the world.
- Plan, prepare, and serve (using available ingredients and technology) specific foods prepared in the style of a variety of ethnic and/or Native cuisines, and draw comparisons among them.
- Correctly use terminology associated with food and nutrition.
- Communicate the results of their inquiries effectively.

In North America, bread is a very common food. A multitude of sandwiches and other food products can be made from any type of bread. The expression "Bread is the staff of life" tells us just how important bread is to our daily lives. Although a loaf of bread may not be so common everywhere, bread and grain products form the basis of many cuisines around the world. Breads are made from the staple grains most abundant in the country or region in which they are grown.

Your Role

You are a local grocery store owner in a community with a diverse population. In order to serve all your customers well, you want to provide bread products that can form the basis of their diet. You also want to provide products that typically accompany the most popular bread products. These dips, soups, stews, spreads, and sauces provide flavour and additional nutrients to the diet. The more accurately you gauge the tastes of different cultural groups, the more profitable your store will be. In order to make your customers aware of the products available, you ask your staff to do some research and create small demonstrations and fact sheets.

Target Group

Within your foods lab group, you are to choose a bread product that is typical of a specific cultural group living in Canada. Examples include corn or wheat tortillas (Mexico and Latin America), *injera* flatbread (many parts of Africa), rye bread (many parts of eastern Europe), rice products (Japan and China), *naan* bread (India), and pasta (Italy). You must select a cultural group, a grain or bread product typical of it, and something to accompany the bread that will add flavour and nutrition.

Food Presentation

- Find a recipe for a grain or bread product typical of your chosen country/region or culture.
- Select something to accompany the bread (e.g., dip, soup, stew, spread, or sauce). This dish should include ingredients typical of the culture.
- Get approval for your recipes from the teacher.
- Make a one-half to one-page fact sheet about the product and the accompaniment. Discuss staple foods, typical flavours (spices and herbs) and why they might be used (geography, climate, historical influence, and so on).
- Include how the food is commonly prepared, served, and eaten.
- You will present your products to the class as if they are potential customers in the grocery store.

Making the Food

1. List the equipment that you will need to prepare the recipe from start to finish.

2. Give your teacher a list of ingredients you need. Your teacher and your group will determine what is already on hand, and what must be purchased, and by whom.

After Each Presentation

Answer the following questions on another sheet of paper.

1. List some common features of the grain products presented by each group.

2. What are the main differences among the grain products presented?

3. In general, what is the nutrient value of the bread products?

4. In general, what are the characteristics of the accompanying foods?

5. How has Canadian cuisine been influenced by the immigration of different peoples? How has the food of other cultures been influenced by Canadian food? Be sure to give examples in your explanations.

Bread and So Much More—Assessment and Evaluation

Category/ Expectations	Criteria	Level 1	Level 2	Level 3	Level 4
Knowledge and Understanding ■ Correctly use terminology associated with world cuisines ■ Identify the components and foods that form the basis of various cuisines around the world. ■ Identify the components of a cuisine (e.g., staple foods, conventions of service and consumption, utensils. ■ Identify the economic, political, and environmental factors that affect food production and supply around the world.	■ Fact sheet/demonstration workshop uses terminology specific to world cuisines. º Staple º Flavours (spices and herbs) º Nutrients ■ Shows how/why the foods chosen are typical of the country/ region or culture. º Environmental º Geographical º Political º Historical				
Thinking and Inquiry ■ Describe a selection of the wide variety of tastes and food preferences displayed by societies around the world.	■ Answers additional questions after the comparison of the different foods.				
Communication ■ Communicate the results of your inquiries effectively.	■ Presents fact sheet and/or demonstration in an organized manner. ■ Uses language suitable for customers. ■ Provides visuals to promote understanding. ■ Uses proper spelling and grammar.				
Application ■ Plan menus for, select, and prepare foods, taking into consideration economic, geographical, and seasonal factors that affect the availability of ingredients. ■ Plan, prepare, and serve specific foods prepared in the style of a variety of ethnic and/or Native cuisines, and draw comparisons among them.	■ Recipe is representative of country/region or culture. ■ Recipe is provided. ■ Grocery list is provided and negotiated. ■ Equipment list is provided and negotiated.				

Name: ____________________ Date: __________ Class: __________

Different Strokes for Different Folks

Consider the following equipment and food related phenomena and how they affect the preparation and/or eating of foods. Brainstorm how they could affect cooking and eating habits, and list foods that are associated with the device or process.

Item	Preparation and and.Eating Customs	Typical Foods
Chopsticks	Most items must be chopped into small pieces	Stir-fried vegetables with rice
Microwave Oven		
Bread Maker		
Clay Oven		
Open Fire		
Utensils (knives, forks, spoons)		
Fast-Food Drive Thru		
Bulk Food Store		

Name: ______________________ Date: __________ Class: __________

STUDY GUIDE **3-7**

Food Security and Hunger

Instructions

Use Chapter 32: Food Security and Hunger (pp. 670–685) to answer the following questions.

Knowledge and Understanding

1. Define the following terms.

Food Security	
FAO	
Spiral of Malnutrition	
World Food Program	

Thinking and Inquiry

2. Even when there is food available, why is food security impossible for some people?

3. List three circumstances that often limit food security in developing countries.

a. ____________________

____

b. ____________________

____

c. ____________________

____

4. How does FAO work to improve food security?

5. How does the SPFS aim to improve food safety?

6. Fill in the following chart about nutrition deficiencies.

Deficiency	Consequences	People Most Affected
Iron		
Vitamin A		
Iodine		

7. What factors contribute to malnutrition?

a. ______________________________

b. ______________________________

c. ______________________________

8. List four different initiatives that aid organizations are implementing to combat malnutrition.

a. ______________________________

b. ______________________________

c. ______________________________

d. ______________________________

9. List five natural disasters that may lead to the need for food aid.

a. ______________________________

b. ______________________________

c. ______________________________

d. ______________________________

e. ______________________________

10. The WFP fights hunger in the following ways:

Action	Description
R	
R	
R	
D	

11. How does education affect hunger?

12. What causes poverty and hunger in Canada?

Name: ______________________ Date: __________ Class: __________

STUDY GUIDE **3-8**

Investigating World Hunger

Instructions

Use Chapter 25: Investigating World Hunger (pp. 512–527) to answer the following questions.

Knowledge and Understanding

1. Define the following terms.

Subsistence Farming	
Cash Crops	
CIDA	
QPM	
CAFB	

2. List five things that the Toronto Food Charter strives to ensure, in a food-secure city.

a. ______________________

b. ______________________

c. ______________________

d. ______________________

e. ______________________

Thinking and Inquiry

3. Rate the community around you. How do you think it meets the criteria for a food-secure community? Consider various target groups in your analysis.

4. What are the advantages and disadvantages of the various types of food aid listed below?

Subsidization	Advantages	Disadvantages
Food Banks		
Community Gardens		
Good Food Box		
Food Access Grants		
Diversion of Food to Food Banks		
Community Kitchens		

5. In the past, corporate development initiatives have donated equipment (tractors, combines, and so on) to various developing countries. However, this usually has not solved the problems of food security. Explain why.

6. Read the article on pages 520-521, "Research Improves Crop Yields, Farmer Income, and Nutrition." Describe how farmers are improving the nutritional status of families.

Name: ______________________ Date: __________ Class: __________

7. According to CIDA's policies, what key factors improve food security?

a. ____

____

b. ____

____

c. ____

____

d. ____

____

8. What three responsibilities was the United Nations given at the World Summit on Sustainable Development in 1996?

a. ____

____

b. ____

____

c. ____

____

Conscientious Chocolate

Jennifer Bain
jbain@thestar.ca
April 7, 2004. 07:33 AM

Here are a few puny thoughts on a complex, global subject.

As Canadian kids hunt for chocolate Easter eggs this weekend, West African children will spray pesticides and wield machetes to harvest cocoa beans used to produce chocolate for the world.

Some of them are young slaves who were sold by desperate parents. Alongside them, women and men will also toil long hours in unsafe conditions.

So what's a conscientious Canadian consumer to do about this ugly chocolate fact? Refusing to indulge isn't a realistic option—we each enjoy about 6.7 kilograms of chocolate annually. And besides, wiping out a major West African economy would devastate the people.
But here are three reasonable things we can all do:
#1: Educate ourselves about global chocolate issues.
#2: Lobby government and chocolate makers for change.
#3: Eat at least some chocolate that's not linked to exploitive work practices.

Save the Children Canada is working hard on the first two points. Knowing consumers are the world's most powerful advocacy group, it is circulating a petition calling for an end to child trafficking and forced child labour in cocoa production, plus asking chocolate manufacturers to start buying cocoa that's free of exploitive forms of child labour.

The goal, says the group's senior analyst Anita Sheth, is "to clear the hazards out of agricultural work" involving kids.

In Ottawa, a company selling certified organic, Fair Trade cocoa, hot chocolate and chocolate bars under the Cocoa Camino label has a different tactic on points 1 through 3.

La Siembra Co-Op believes paying a fair price for cocoa is the way to win ideal working conditions for all. While 70 per cent of the world's cocoa supply comes from West Africa, where 10 million people live on cocoa farms, La Siembra buys from co-operatives of family farms in the Dominican Republic.

The Fair Trade certification tells consumers that farmers receive higher than world market prices. The organic certification means better health for farmers, the environment and consumers. "It's about baby steps," says co-director Jeff de Jong.

According to de Jong, each Canadian eats about five 100-gram chocolate bars a month. "If every chocolate-consuming Canadian was to purchase just one of those five 100-gram bars each month as certified Fair Trade, this would translate into a 20 per cent chocolate market share for Fair Trade."

Eventually, multinational chocolate manufacturers would create similar lines to cash in on the lucrative Fair Trade market.

Hmm, seems like a win-win way out of an intolerable situation. Still, there's much to be said and done on what has been dubbed "the beans of bondage."

Ethical Chocolate Cake

Find Cocoa Camino organic, Fair Trade cocoa and sugar in grocery and health food stores. The cocoa comes with this vegan recipe, adapted from the *Moosewood Restaurant Book of Desserts.*

1-1/2 cups unbleached white or all-purpose flour
1/3 cup organic, Fair Trade cocoa powder
1 tsp baking soda
1/2 tsp sea salt
1 cup organic, Fair Trade sugar
1/2 cup vegetable oil
1 cup cold water or coffee
2 tsp pure vanilla extract
2 tbsp apple cider vinegar

- Sift or stir together flour, cocoa, baking soda, salt, and sugar in ungreased, 8-inch square baking pan.
- In large measuring cup, mix oil, water or coffee, and vanilla. Pour into flour mixture, mixing with fork until smooth. Stir in vinegar just until evenly distributed. (As it reacts to the baking soda, it will cause pale swirls in batter.)
- Bake in preheated 375F oven 25 to 30 minutes, or until cake springs back when lightly pressed in centre.
- Cool thoroughly in pan on wire rack.

Makes 9 servings.

For more information on Fair Trade, try the following web sites:
Make Trade Fair: http://www.maketradefair.com/en/index.htm
Oxfam Canada: http://www.oxfam.ca/campaigns/fairTrade.htm
New Internationalist Magazine (Fair Trade):
http://www.newint.org/issue322/contents.htm?OVRAW=Fair%20Trade&OVKEY=fair%20trade&OVMTC=standard

Answer the following questions on a separate sheet of paper.

1. Why do you think the Fair Trade project was initiated in the Dominican Republic rather than West Africa?
2. Investigate Save the Children Canada and explain the organization's objectives and/or mandate. Highlight the issues that the organization addresses
3. Bono (of the rock group U2) recently petitioned Western nations to forgive debt owed by developing countries. Investigate the issue of the debt drain. Explain how Bono's proposal may help developing countries.
4. Write a letter to a chocolate bar manufacturer to highlight the issues mentioned in this article. Explain the challenges that families face when producing cash crops.

Name: ______________________ Date: __________ Class: __________

3-10

FOOD LAB

Food: A Limited Resource

Specific Expectations

- Describe economic factors that have an impact on the food choices of individuals and families.
- Plan menus for, select, and prepare foods, taking into consideration economic, geographical, and seasonal factors that affect the availability of ingredients.
- Identify the source of nutrients and the role they play in the maintenance of good health.
- Demonstrate an understanding of the nutrients provided by foods in each category of Canada's Food Guide to Healthy Eating and other dietary guides and standards, and using this knowledge, describe ways to achieve healthy body weight and body image.
- Describe ways of preparing and storing food to provide for maximum nutrient retention.
- Demonstrate how to use equipment correctly to prepare and store foods for maximum nutrient retention (e.g., steamer, pressure cooker, freezer).
- Use available resources, including computer technology, both to plan a menu consisting of foods that will maintain good health, and to select and prepare those foods..
- Identify the ways in which the local community is responding to hunger and food security (e.g., with food banks, community gardens).
- Correctly use terminology associated with food and nutrition.
- Communicate the results of their inquiries effectively.

Not everyone in Canada is food secure. Many people in our own communities cannot afford good quality food to maintain a healthy active life. As a result, there are programs and facilities to help provide these people with some good quality food. The programs available vary according to community. See Chapter 25: Investigating Hunger to review some of the programs available in some communities.

Your Role

You are a member of a recipe development team. Your most recent contract was developing a booklet with a set of recipes and nutrition information for people who have limited access to food and depend on subsidization programs to meet their food needs. You know what is available in the community, so your job is to develop tasty, nutritious and simple recipes that use the products people know they will receive through various organizations. Since you know the resources are limited, you are to provide helpful hints and tips to encourage people to try different things.

FOOD: A LIMITED RESOURCE, *continued*

Target Group

Your target group is people in the community who cannot afford enough good quality food. This could be due to several factors including job loss, being a single-parent family, or being new immigrants.

Your Food Product

Find a recipe or develop a recipe that uses foods typically found at a food bank. Although you may use a limited number of other foods, the basics should be among the products found in the food bank.

The recipe should feed a family of four.

Your recipe should include various food groups. If the recipe itself does not use all the food groups, provide meal/menu suggestions for how to make it more nutritious.

Making the Food

List the equipment that you will need to prepare the recipe from start to finish.

Provide your teacher with a list of ingredients needed. Your teacher and your group will determine what is already on hand, and what must be purchased and by whom.

Answer the following questions on a separate sheet of paper.

1. Show your calculations for costing out the meal for a family of four.
2. Investigate in your community or through the Internet what foods are usually distributed in a food bank.
3. In order to encourage better nutrition, what additions would you make to food bank foods?
4. Buying in bulk is a way to help reduce costs, but it is not always possible, especially for families on a limited income. Explain why.

Name: ______________________ Date: __________ Class: __________

Food: A Limited Resource Assessment and Evaluation

Category/Expectations	Criteria	Level 4	Level 3	Level 2	Level 1
Knowledge and Understanding ■ Describe economic factors that have an impact on the food choices of individuals and families. ■ Identify the source of nutrients and the role they play in the maintenance of good health. ■ Correctly use terminology associated with local food security.	■ Foods are typical of those donated to a food bank ■ Recognizes the nutrients within the recipe and/or meal ° Food groups. ° Nutrients.				
Thinking and Inquiry ■ Identify the ways in which the local community is responding to hunger and food security (e.g., with food banks, community gardens). ■ Describe ways of preparing and storing food to provide for maximum nutrient retention.	■ Community programs ° Lists existing programs. ° Suggests improvements. ■ Provides suggestions on how to improve a family's food security. ■ Provides additional suggestions for varied cooking methods for maintaining nutrients.				
Communication ■ Communicate the results of inquiries effectively.	■ Presents fact sheet and/or demonstration in an organized manner. ■ Uses language suitable for customers. ■ Provides visuals to promote understanding. ■ Uses proper spelling and grammar.				
Application ■ Plan menus for, select, and prepare foods,taking into consideration economic, geographical, and seasonal factors that affect the availability of ingredients. ■ Use available resources, including computer technology, both to plan a menu consisting of foods that will maintain good health, and to select and prepare those foods.	■ Provides recipe. ■ Provides and negotiates grocery list. ■ Provides and negotiates equipment list. ■ Provides costing for meal for family of four.				

Name: ______________________ Date: __________ Class: __________

Social Science Research —Food Insecurity through Another's Eyes

3-11

Specific Expectations

- Identify the economic, political, and environmental factors that affect food production and supply throughout the world.
  - ° Describe the effects of various economic factors on food production and supply (e.g., standards of living, poverty, personal and family incomes, employment and unemployment).
- Identify the factors that are critical to achieving and maintaining food security and eliminating hunger.
  - ° Describe the social and cultural traditions that account for inequality among peoples of the world (e.g., gender issues, distribution of wealth, failure to support small business).
  - ° Identify the ways in which the local community is responding to hunger and food security (e.g., with food banks, community gardens).
- Use appropriate Social Science research methods in the investigation of food-related issues/
- Communicate the results of their inquiries effectively

Your Role

You are a Social Science researcher who is investigating the issues of food insecurity in your local community or another part of the world. You want to know how a particular organization is helping to alleviate hunger and its effects. Choose a person working in such an organization and describe the skill and other qualifications for his/her job.

To Accomplish These Tasks

1. Choose a person working in an organization that helps alleviate the effects of food insecurity. This could be in your own community. Some examples include:
   - A manager of a food bank.
   - A planner for a community garden.
   - A cook in a community kitchen.
   - Students who have organized a school food drive.
   - A dietitian with public health department.
   - A volunteer or social worker who works with the immigrant or ESL population.
   - A church administrator whose parish donates food or money within the community or to missionaries in the developing world.
   - Another idea approved by the teacher.

Alternatively, you may develop a survey to investigate the perceptions people have of hunger within a community.

2. Develop an interview or a survey based on your specific topic.
   a. Provide a title for your topic.
   b. Develop an introduction to explain your purpose to the sample group. Ensure confidentiality.
   c. Write a survey or a set of interview questions. You should have 10–15 questions relating to the topic of food insecurity in the community.
      i. Interview questions should be open-ended. They should not direct the interviewee to any particular answer, and should require detailed responses. Additional questions may be asked during the interview to clarify or provide more depth.
      ii. Survey questions should be closed. They should supply answers that produce detailed information about the issues. If written answers are required, they should be very brief.
      iii. You should conduct one in-depth interview. If you are completing a survey, you should gather at least 15–30 sets of answers.

3. Conduct the interview or survey. Collect the information, collate, organize, and interpret the results.

4. Write a brief report summarizing the results of your survey.

Name: ______________________ Date: __________ Class: __________

Food Insecurity Through Another's Eyes Assessment and Evaluation

Category/ Expectations	Criteria	Level 1	Level 2	Level 3	Level 4
Knowledge and Understanding ■ Identify the economic, political, and environmental factors that affect food production and supply throughout the world. ■ Describe the social and cultural traditions that account for inequality among peoples of the world. ■ Describe the effects of various economic factors on food production and supply (e.g., standards of living, poverty, personal and family incomes, employment and unemployment). ■ Identify the factors that are critical to achieving and maintaining food security and eliminating hunger.	■ Uses interview or survey questions to investigate some of the following causes of hunger: ° Economic ° Political ° Environmental ° Social ° Cultural or gender-based inequities. ■ Asks questions to investigate the effects and impact of living in poverty. ■ Asks questions to identify how the activity or organization is working to combat hunger.				
Thinking and Inquiry ■ Use appropriate Social Science research methods in the investigation of food related issues.	■ Stated topic ■ Introduction. ■ Survey or interview results collected, collated, and interpreted.				
Communication ■ Communicate the results of their inquiries effectively	■ Uses proper spelling and grammar. ■ Is clear in presentation. ■ Organizes in small report format.				
Application ■ identify the ways in which the local community is responding to hunger and food security (e.g., with food banks, community gardens)	■ Chooses appropriate sample group. ■ Chooses appropriate organization.				

Unit 3 Test Bank

Note: The teacher may use these questions to devise a test suitable to the exact content covered and the students' experiences. The questions may be given in a traditional test format and/or some indication of the questions could be given to students beforehand to facilitate additional research.

1. Staple foods are:
- **a.** Foods that are required to be eaten every day by the people in an area.
- **b.** Foods that are grown largely for export and the money they bring in.
- **c.** The main foods that comprise the diet of most of the people in an area.
- **d.** Foods that should not be eaten after one has had stomach-stapling surgery.

2. The staple foods of poorer counties usually consist of:
- **a.** Fish and/or poultry.
- **b.** Meat products.
- **c.** Rice and/or wheat.
- **d.** None of the above.

3. An extreme scarcity of the food needed for a healthy life is referred to as:
- **a.** Undernutrition.
- **b.** Food security.
- **c.** Famine.
- **d.** Mortality rate.

4. Always having access to the food needed for a healthy lifestyle is:
- **a.** Overnutrition.
- **b.** Food security.
- **c.** Food policy.
- **d.** Commodity food.

5. A crop that is typical of a country or area, but is largely sold for export is:
- **a.** A commodity food.
- **b.** Food policy.
- **c.** Free trade.
- **d.** A cash crop.

6. Which of the following nutrients are most often deficient in the diets of people in developing nations?
- **a.** Phosphorus and magnesium.
- **b.** Vitamin A and iron.
- **c.** Vitamins C and D.
- **d.** Vitamins E and K.

7. How can culture impact hunger problems?
- **a.** People may be missing nutrients because the only food sources are forbidden by the culture
- **b.** People may be unable to harvest available food using traditional tools.
- **c.** People may go hungry in a vegetarian culture.
- **d.** People may not produce enough food when the land is dry and non-workable.

8 Which statement is a hunger myth?
a. Some groups of people profit from keeping people hungry.
b. Technology does not help poor people who lack the resources to buy it.
c. There is not enough food in the world to feed the hungry.
d. When people work together for solutions at the grassroots level, change can happen.

9. Which region typically uses mostly wheat?
a. Africa.
b. Asia.
c. Central America.
d. Eastern Europe.

10. A staple food that is very low in protein, but suitable because many can easily grow it in many places:
a. Corn.
b. Rice.
c. Wheat.
d. Potatoes.

11. The growing and eating of corn/maize is most typical of which country?
a. Ecuador.
b. Canada.
c. India.
d. Denmark.

12. The growing and eating of rice is most typical of which country?
a. Germany.
b. Sudan.
c. Congo.
d. Sierra Leone.

13. The growing and eating of roots and tubers are typical of which region?
a. Western Europe.
b. Middle East.
c. Parts of Africa.
d. Southern Europe.

14. Animal products as a staple food are typical of:
a. North America.
b. Central and South America.
c. Western Europe.
d. All of the above

15. Which of the following is true about herbs?
a. Tend to be brownish in colour.
b. Tend to be cool flavours.
c. Are generally berries, seeds, or bark of plants.
d. Tend to be hot flavours.

16. Cumin is:
a. Used in curry powders, chutney, and pickles.
b. Has a sweet flavour.
c. Is a herb.
d. All of the above.

17. Ginger
a. Has a hot, pungent, spicy flavour.
b. It typical in many Asian dishes.
c. Is a spice.
d. All of the above.

18. The main producer of cocoa is:
a. North America.
b. West and Central Africa.
c. Europe.
d. Asia.

19. Natural disasters influencing hunger include:
a. Drought.
b. Media publications.
c. Debt repayments.
d. Lack of education

20. Fufu is most common for which regions of the world?
a. North America.
b. South and Central America.
c. Sub-Saharan Africa.
d. Southeast Asia.

21. Polenta is a grain product most common in which region of the world?
a. Southern Europe.
b. Middle East.
c. Eastern Europe.
d. All of the above.

22. Iodine deficiency has been drastically reduced by the use of:
a. Supplements for breastfeeding mothers.
b. Iodized salt.
c. Providing infection control through public health.
d. None of the above.

23. Which country's peoples spend the largest percentage of their income on food?
a. Canada.
b. Germany.
c. Greece.
d. India.

24. Which of the following would be considered a cash crop?
a. Millet.
b. Meat.
c. Chocolate.
d. Corn.

25. The main cause of hunger in the world today is:
a. Overpopulation.
b. Poverty.
c. Natural disasters.
d. All of the above.

26. This grain is more easily grown in areas prone to drought in the United States and Canada; it is used for animal feed rather than food for people.
a. Corn.
b. Sorghum.
c. Wheat.
d. Potatoes.

Thinking and Inquiry

27. Design a graphic organizer to show the connections among concepts related to food security. (Use words, diagrams, web or bubble diagram, etc.)
- °. Incorporate factors that influence food security.
- ° Include several issues that are local and global. Explain the connections between factors.
- ° Clearly explain the sphere of influence (household, community, provincial/federal, and international/political).

Application

28. You are a Red Cross/Red Crescent international development worker who has been sent to a developing country to work in a program alleviating hunger. This is the second or third developing country you have visited. Write a letter home describing the issues associated with hunger in the country you are in, but compare the situation to the previous countries and Canada as well.
- ■ Describe the flavours and typical dishes of the countries.
  - ° Herbs and spices.
  - ° Staple foods.
- ■ Give examples of equipment used to prepare and eat the food.
- ■ Compare the hunger and poverty situations in the three developing countries to those in Canada.
- ■ Incorporate specific examples of programs (real or imagined) that help.

29. You are a director for a non-governmental organization that is applying for grants (from the Canadian International Developmental Agency) to implement a program to alleviate hunger. You have picked one or two of your best proposals to present. For each:
- ° Choose a country or region for your focus.
- ° Detail the general needs of the people of the country (including different racial, ethnic, gender, and age groups).
- ° Describe how your plan will be implemented.
- ° Explain what you expect your results to be and how you will measure the results to determine the effectiveness of your program.

Communication

30. You have just been hired for the Food Network. Your show will travel the world and document the typical foods and customs of various cultures. You have already researched your first three to four locations. Provide an overview of your first three to four programs. Include the following:
- ■ Flavours in the form of herbs and spices.
- ■ Customs in preparing, serving, and eating foods.
- ■ Staple foods and cash crops.
- ■ Variations in Canada.

Name: ______________________ Date: __________ Class: __________

3-13

CULMINATING ACTIVITY

Careers—A Chef's Tour

You Eat What You Are

You are an executive chef at a school that trains future chefs. Chefs have highly marketable skills and chefs are recruited and employed to travel and work around the world. These future chefs will be seeking careers in numerous parts of the world, cooking for people of various religions, cultures, and socio-economic classes. In order to meet the needs of their future clients, it is important for these chefs to understand the native foods and food customs associated with the cultures in which they will work.

Specific Expectations

- Identify the social, psychological, economic, emotional, cultural, religious, and physical factors that affect food choices.
- Identify examples of entrepreneurship in the food industry, and occupations related to food and nutrition sciences.
- Identify the components and foods that form the basis of various cuisines around the world.
- Identify the components of a cuisine (e.g., staple foods, conventions of service and consumption, utensils)
- Identify the economic, political, and environmental factors that affect food production and supply throughout the world.
- Describe the effects of various economic factors on food production and supply (e.g., standards of living, poverty, personal and family incomes, employment and unemployment).
- Identify current food crises (e.g., contamination, crop failures), the factors causing each of them (e.g., production increases, unfavourable global weather changes), and their impact on the availability and cost of food.
- Identify the factors that are critical to achieving and maintaining food security and eliminating hunger.
- Correctly use the terminology of food and nutrition sciences (e.g., *nutrient deficiencies, food security, vegetarianism, cuisine, agribusiness, gluten development*).
- Effectively communicate the results of their inquiries, using a variety of methods and forms (e.g., graphs, charts, diagrams, oral presentations, written reports, videos).

Oral Presentation:

Part A

1. Choose a recipe that is typical of a particular country or region of a country. You should use a number of different ingredients. List and describe each ingredient and provide complete instructions on how to prepare the recipe.

2. Highlight the staple foods of the country and use other foods typical of the region. In your recipe you should also consider and use any cash crops grown for export.

3. Describe the typical flavours of the dishes prepared in the country. Discuss the favourite herbs, spices, and other flavourings and where they might be imported from if not grown locally.

4. Describe how the foods typically are prepared and with what types of equipment. Indicate any customs and/or habits associated with preparation and serving.

Part B

5. Discuss the main issues associated with hunger and food distribution in the country or other similar countries. You should consider the factors stated in Chapter 25: Investigating World Hunger, including economics, fuel shortages, overpopulation, war and politics, and natural disasters. Investigate historical and recent issues related to the general food security in the country/region and/or how it might affect other countries.

Some Helpful Hints

- Try to present the recipe and other information to the student chefs in an interesting way. Remember, they will be working with food the rest of their lives. It is important for them to understand all the issues around it.
- Create your own organization and presentation style—there is no right or wrong—but present the information creatively and clearly.
- Use pictures or symbols to make foods meaningful and memorable. Remember that much of the appeal of food is in its appearance.
- You may want to draw some samples of the foods: herbs, spices, and staples. You could even bring in the real thing to show students during your presentation.
- Be organized and neat when presenting both foods and information.
- The teacher might ask you to make a sample of the recipe, so be well prepared.
- Be sure you observe food safety rules for preparing and storing ingredients.

Name: ____________________ Date: __________ Class: __________

Category/ Expectations	Criteria	Level 1	Level 2	Level 3	Level 4
Knowledge and Understanding ■ Correctly use terminology of food and nutrition sciences.	■ Uses correct terminology for: ° Staple and cash crop foods ° Flavours (herbs and spices) ° Equipment, common practices, customs, etiquette, etc. ° Food security ° Concepts associated with hunger, etc.				
Thinking and Inquiry ■ Identify the social, psychological, economic, emotional, cultural, religious, and physical factors that affect food choices. ■ Identify the components of a cuisine (e.g., staple foods, conventions of service and consumption, utensils). ■ Identify the components and foods that form the basis of various cuisines around the world.	■ Chooses recipe(s) and foods that are representative of the country/region including: ° Staple food(s) ° Flavours (herbs and spices) ° Preparation ° Customs and habits ° Issues related to hunger.				
Communication ■ Effectively communicate the results of your inquiries, using a variety of methods and forms (e.g., graphs, charts, diagrams, oral presentations, written reports, videos)	■ Uses proper spelling and grammar ■ Presents in a neat and attractive fashion ■ Uses graphics, visuals, or samples to convey the lesson to students: ° Food(s) ° Map(s) ° Staples and/or spices. ° Techniques of preparation ° Customs/habits ° People				
Application ■ Identify examples of entrepreneurship in the food industry, and occupations related to food and nutrition sciences.	■ Relates information to the occupation of chef. ■ Teaches chefs about foods of the world.				

Name: ______________________ Date: __________ Class: __________

Unit 4: Contemporary Issues in Food

4-1

What You Need to Know	Where to Find It
■ Examine the current state of agriculture in Canada ■ Identify the factors that impact on food production ■ Examine the role of food additives in the production of food items ■ Identify legislation governing additive use ■ Examine the role of pesticides and fertilizers in the production and supply of food ■ Investigate environmental issues in agriculture	■ Ch. 31: Factors affecting food production and supply (pp. 647–653) ■ Ch. 16: (pp. 327–334) o Food Science Lab Preservatives in Bread o Ice Cream Lab ■ Ch. 31: (pp. 653–658) ■ Ch. 31: (pp. 658–660) o What is "sustainable" agriculture?
■ Identify the impact of biotechnology on food production and safety ■ Investigate careers in agriculture and food science	■ Ch. 31: (pp. 662–665) Issues in Biotechnology—Letter to the Editor ■ Ch. 6: Public Health Inspector (pp. 99) ■ Ch. 31: Associate Professor of Plant Agriculture (pp. 667) ■ Careers in Agriculture (Interview)
■ Examine factors that affect food market trends ■ Describe new developments in food production, preparation, and services ■ Examine the role of organic foods in the diet ■ Examine current trends in food packaging technology	■ Ch. 29:(pp. 605–606) ■ Ch. 29 (pp. 606–615) ■ Ch. 29 (pp. 616–618) ■ Ch. 29 (pp. 621) o Comparing Organic and Non-Organic Foods Lab ■ Ch. 29 (pp. 618–620) o Food Packaging Technology
■ Unit 4 Culminating Activity-Prepare a position paper on a present-day issue related to food and nutrition	■ Contemporary Issues in Food Position Paper
	■ Supplemental Information Ch. 24 Canadian Food Supply and Production

Name: ______________________ Date: __________ Class: __________

4-2

DIAGNOSTIC QUIZ

Unit 4: Diagnostic Quiz

Multiple Choice

1. Before using a new food additive a manufacturer must make an application to Health Canada. The manufacturer must submit the following information before receiving approval:
   a. Results of safety tests.
   b. Explanation of how the additive will be used.
   c. Benefits of the additive to the consumer.
   d. All of the above.

2. There are currently more than _________ additives approved for use in Canada.
   a. 1000.
   b. 2000.
   c. 3000.
   d. 5000.

3. Which of the following changes in Canadian society is impacting the food being produced and marketed?
   a. The aging of the baby boom.
   b. Smaller families.
   c. Increasingly diverse ethnic population.
   d. More dual-career families.
   e. All of the above.

4. Answer true or false to each of the following statements:

   ________ 72 percent of Canadians state that when making food choices, nutrition is important.

   ________ 65 percent of consumers are very or somewhat concerned about the amount of fat in their diets.

   ________ 75 percent of Canadians have changed or improved their eating habits to maintain their personal health.

   ________ The most common changes in eating habits are as follows: 34 percent of surveyed Canadians consumed less fat, 26 percent ate more fruits and vegetables, and 14 percent reduce their sugar intake.

5. Match the term on the left with its definition on the right. Each term will be used only once. All terms will be used.

____ Functional food	**a.** product that is sold in medical form, not associated with food.
____ Nutraceutical	**b.** formed in the body as a result of normal metabolism, circulate around the body causing damage.
____ Antioxidants	**c.** food that has physical benefits and/or reduces the risk of chronic disease.
_____ Free radicals	**d.** help to reduce the damage caused by free radicals before they cause damage.

6. Texturized vegetable protein:
- **a.** Is obtained from eggs.
- **b.** Is sold wet and can be dehydrated.
- **c.** Has a texture similar to chicken.
- **d.** Can be used to replace ground meat in chili, tacos, and lasagna.

7. Which of the following are herbs?
- **a.** Basil, thyme, peppercorns, sage.
- **b.** Oregano, rosemary, sage, bay leaf.
- **c.** Nutmeg, peppercorns, cinnamon, cumin.
- **d.** Chili powder, curry powder, oregano, bay leaf.

8. True or False: Breakfast is the food-service industry's fastest growing segment.

9. List four new developments in food packaging technology.

a. ______________________________

____

b. ______________________________

____

c. ______________________________

____

d. ______________________________

____

10. Which of the following statements are true about organic foods? Choose all that apply.
- **a.** There is an increase in the availability of organically produced foods in grocery stores and markets.
- **b.** Organic foods are more nutritious than their non-organic counterparts.
- **c.** Organic foods are usually similar in price to their non-organic counterparts.
- **d.** Organic farmers use composted matter and manure to fertilize their crops.

11. True or False: Farms are decreasing in size.

12. Identify four ways farmers control pests.

    a. ______________________________

    b. ______________________________

    c. ______________________________

    d. ______________________________

13. What is bioengineering?

14. True or False: The government carefully monitors products derived from biotechnology.

15. What is aquaculture? Give examples of foods that are produced through this method.

Name: ______________________ Date: __________ Class: __________

STUDY GUIDE

4-3

Factors Affecting Food Production and Supply

Refer to pages 646– to 667 to complete the following questions.

Knowledge and Understanding

1. Define the following terms.

Net Income Stabilization Account (NISA)	
Canadian Farm Income Program (CFIP)	
Pesticides	
Pest Management Regulatory Agency (PMRA)	
Integrated Pest Management (IPM)	
Fertilizers	
Canadian Food Inspection Agency (CFIA)	
Bioengineering	
Cell switch	
Aquaculture	
Department of Fisheries and Oceans (DFO)	
Sustainable development	

Thinking and Inquiry

2. Create an organizer that details how farms have changed over the past 30 years. Address the following factors: farm size, number of people farming, farm ownership, land ownership, who is farming the land, computer use, variety of skills needed, farm income, costs vs. gate prices. You may choose to do this in the form of graphs, charts, a mind map, or a timeline. Complete this question on a separate sheet of paper.

3. What is the impact of urban development on the price of agricultural land? What are the consequences to both farmers and consumers of increasing land costs?

4. List and describe the methods used by farmers to control pests.

5. True or False: The pesticides used by today's farmers are more likely to cause harm to the land and food it produces than in the past. Explain your response.

6. Why do farmers use fertilizers?

7. To reduce the use of fertilizers on land, what processes have been implemented by both government and farmers?

8. Explain how tillage practices help to conserve soil.

9. What role does manure play in the sustainability of agriculture? Describe how farmers are combating the odour produced by manure.

10. List and explain three different ways in which farmers and Health Canada ensure that the food produced in Canada is safe to eat.

a. ____

____

b. ____

____

c. ____

____

Communication

11. Identify and describe three goals of bioengineering and biotechnology.

12. Explain the processes that have been put in place by the Canadian government to ensure that the foods derived through biotechnology are safe to eat.

13. List the 4 four guidelines for labelling of genetically modified food in Canada.

14. Complete the following chart, identifying both the positive and negative aspects of aquaculture.

Positives	Negatives

Food Additives

Refer to pages 327–334 to complete the following questions.

Knowledge and Understanding

1. Define the following terms.

Food additives	
Food and Drugs Act	
Phenylketonuria	
Centre of Science in the Public Interest	
Aspartame	
Olestra	
Caffeine	
Food fortification	

2. Outline the steps taken by Health Canada to ensure that food additives are safe.

3. Explain why it is important to be informed about food additives from a health perspective. Give two specific examples to support your explanation.

Thinking and Inquiry

4. Select five food products. Read the ingredients lists and then complete the following chart identifying the additives used in the product, the purpose of each additive, and list any specific claims made on the label about the additives used in the product.

Food Product	Additives Listed	Purpose of Additive	Claims about Additives

Name: ______________________ Date: __________ Class: __________

4-5

FOOD LAB

Learning about Preservatives

By comparing slices of store-bought bread containing preservatives to homemade bread that contains no preservatives, you can learn about the role of preservatives in food and how they act to slow down decomposition.

Procedure:

1. Place one slice of each type of bread on a plate, uncovered.
2. Allow each slice of bread to sit on the counter for 10 minutes.
3. Using a water dropper, dot each slice of bread with 10 drops of water. Be careful to drop the same amount of water on each slice of bread.
4. Cover each slice of bread with plastic wrap. Label each slice as "preservatives" or "no preservatives."
5. Over the next week observe the bread samples and complete the following observation chart. Do not remove the plastic wrap. You may wish to use a magnifying glass to help you gather more specific observations. Ensure that your observations are detailed—record information about the texture, the development of mould, how many spots, and other signs of spoilage.

Based on the procedures above, what do you predict will happen to each slice of bread? How will the slices differ in the reaction to their environment?

Time	Observations
Day One	
Day Three	
Day Five	
Day Seven	

Conclusions

1. Which slice changed texture first? How many days did it take?

2. Which slice developed mould first? How many days did it take?

3. Were they any other signs of spoilage? What were they?

4. How did the plastic wrap affect the results? Why?

5. Refer to the ingredients list for the store-bought bread and the recipe for the homemade bread. Identify any additives used. Which of these additives has a preservative function? You may need to refer to pages 333–334 of *Food for Today, First Canadian Edition*, or the Health Canada web site at www.hc-sc.gc.ca/food-aliment/friia-raaii/food_drugs-aliments_drogues/act-loi/pdf/e_c-tables.pdf.

6. What conclusions can you draw about the use of preservatives in bread based on the results of this experiment? How do preservatives affect the availability of food to consumers?

Name: ______________________ Date: __________ Class: __________

4-6

FOOD LAB

Ice Cream

Ice cream: A wonderful cold treat on a hot summer day. In 2002, Canadian processors made 292.1 million litres of hard ice cream and 17 million litres of soft ice cream! That year, ice cream sales reached $443.5 million.

The main ingredients of ice cream are milk, sugar, eggs, and flavouring. A variety of milk products can be used; for example, cream, whole milk, condensed milk and instant skim-milk powder. Milks with a higher fat content produce a richer, smoother, and more flavourful product. Sugar is commonly used as a sweetener. It increases the palatability and improves the body and texture. Stabilizers such as gelatin may be used to help absorb some of the free water in the ice cream mix and help prevent the formation of large crystals in the ice cream. Gelatin also gives substance and a less watery taste. Eggs help to combine the fat and water and also improve the whipping ability, which results in greater resistance to melting. Although vanilla is the most popular flavour, others can be added to suit your taste.

Hints for Making Good Ice Cream

1. If the ice cream is very soft, the brine is not cold enough. Add more salt to reduce the brine temperature.
2. If the ice cream is coarse in less than 20 minutes, the brine has become too cold too quickly. Too much salt has been used.
3. Make the ice cream mix the day before it will be frozen to get a smoother product and a higher yield.
4. Electric freezing takes longer than hand operated
5. Use crushed ice for freezing.
6. Add liquid flavours before freezing, but add any fruits or nuts after freezing and before hardening.
7. Use a whisk to blend ingredients for best results.
8. Clean the salt off all parts of the freezer before serving.

Why use salt? The concept of melting ice with salt is not new to anyone living in Canada. During the winter months we use salt on our roads, driveways, and sidewalks. As salt is applied to ice, a concentrated brine solution forms on the ice. The freezing point of a 20 percent solution of salt is –16.6ºC. As a result, more ice melts to dilute this solution, until the freezing point of the solution matches the outside temperature (equilibrium is established).

(**Source**: Finding Science in Ice Cream—An Experiment for Secondary School Classrooms, http://www.foodsci.uoguelph.ca/dairyedu/findsci.html. Retrieved July 5, 2004.)

Ice Cream Recipe (makes enough for three to four students)

250 ml (1/2 cup) homogenized milk
125 ml (1/4 cup) sugar
Egg substitute (equivalent to one egg, according to package directions).
2 ml (1/2 tsp) teaspoon vanilla
250 ml (1/2 cup) whipping cream
175 ml (1/3 cup) coarse salt
Crushed ice
Medium-sized zipper-type freezer bag
Large-sized zipper-type freezer bag

NOTE: Do not use raw egg in this recipe. Raw eggs can contain bacteria that may cause illness.

1. Place the milk, sugar, egg substitute, vanilla, and cream into the medium-sized freezer bag. Zip the bag.
2. Place the medium-sized bag in the large bag and pack crushed ice between them. Pour some of the salt evenly over the ice. Continue with the ice and salt until the smaller bag is completely covered. Zip up the large bag.
3. Shake the mixture until it firms up and turns to ice cream. This may take 10 to 15 minutes. You may want to wear gloves because your hands will get *very* cold.
4. Remove the smaller bag from the larger one and wash the small bag under cold running water to remove all traces of salt. Open carefully and enjoy!!

NOTE: This recipe can also be made using two tin cans: a smaller can (similar to a coffee tin) and a larger can. Unused paint cans are great for this and can be purchased from most paint stores. Roll the paint can back and forth, and check the consistency of your ice cream after 15 minutes. If necessary, pour out the water and add more ice and salt. You may also use an electric or hand-cranked ice cream freezer.

Based on the procedures above, what predictions can you make about how the homemade ice cream will compare with commercially prepared ice cream?

Observations

1. Complete the following chart comparing homemade ice cream with commercially-prepared ice cream.

Ice Cream Qualities	Homemade	Commercially-Prepared
Colour		
Texture		
Flavour		
Melting (speed)		

2. Compare the ingredients in homemade ice cream with those in commercially-prepared ice cream. How are they similar? How do they differ?

3. Refer to the ingredients list for the commercially prepared ice cream. Identify any additives used. What is the purpose of each of the additives? You may want to refer to page 333–334 of your text, *Food for Today, First Canadian Edition* or the Health Canada web site at http://www.hc-sc.gc.ca/food-aliment/friia-raaii/food_drugs-aliments_drogues/act-loi/pdf/e_c-tables.pdf. Use the search feature to help you to locate the different additives.

4. Based on your observations, what conclusions can you draw about the use of additives in commercial ice cream? How can additives affect the quality of food consumers buy?

Name: ______________________ Date: __________ Class: __________

4-7

Environmental Issues in Agriculture—What Is "Sustainable" Agriculture?

Specific Expectations

- Describe the effects of various economic factors on food production and supply
- Investigate the impact of a variety of political factors on food quality, production and supply
- Demonstrate an understanding of the effects of different environmental factors and issues on the production and supply of food items
- Identify current food crises, the factors causing each of them and their impact on the availability and cost of food
- Effectively communicate the results of their inquiries, using a variety of methods and forms

Environmentally sustainable agricultural practices recognize our need for the production of food and the development of new and innovative products within an environment that includes not only our natural areas but also our resources such as soil, water, crops, livestock, trees, fish, landscap-landscape and people. Sustainability can be divided into three areas:

1. Environmental sustainability: What practices are used in agriculture to ensure that our soil is fertile, water is safe, and that pests are controlled? Are customers willing to pay more for their food in order to ensure that we produce a safe and abundant supply of food?
2. Economic sustainability: Can farmers survive on the income they generate? Can farmers realize a fair price for their food? Economic sustainability is a matter of supply and demand. If supply is too great, the price will fall and farmers will have a tough time making ends meet.
3. Social sustainability: Farming should enhance the quality of life for both farmers and society. Over the past 70 years there has been a decrease in the number of farms from 729,000 in 1931 to 247,000 in 2001, although the average size of farms has increased dramatically from 91 hectares (227 acres) in 1931 to 273 (674 acres) hectares in 2001. Can a farmer earn a good living and live in a thriving rural community?

Your Task:

You have been asked by the Canadian Federation of Agriculture to create an advertising campaign that informs the Canadian public about sustainable agriculture. Choose one area of sustainability as addressed above and create a public service announcement.

Your announcement should:

- Educate about the sustainability issues.
- Present the dangers; what will happen if we don't address these issues soon?
- Include names of agencies and resources where more information can be obtained.

Your PSA may be done in the form of a billboard, radio or television spot, magazine advertisement, web site, or any other creative way you choose.

You are also required to prepare a media release. A media release is produced by the organization that has responsibility for the PSA. The media release will address the following:

- The name of your PSA campaign.
- The date it will be launched and how long it will run.
- The purpose of the PSA campaign.
- Your goals: Who is your audience?
- The importance of this campaign.
- Why do we need to educate the public about sustainability issues.
- Statistics and research to provide support for the campaign.
- What is unique about your campaign.
- Resources for more information (web sites, agencies books etc).
- What else is being done during the campaign (although you are responsible for producing only one PSA, you may have plans to include other types within the campaign).

Remember that the media release will be given to those working in the media (e.g., journalists, researchers, TV reporters etc.); therefore, direct your release to them.

Suggested Web Sites to Get You Started:

- Canadian Federation of Agriculture www.cfa-fca.ca
- Environmentally sustainable agricultural practices on Prince Edward Island at www.peisland.com/agrtour/intro.html
- Agriculture and Agri-Food Canada http://www.agr.gc.ca/environ_e.phtml

Name: ______________________ Date: __________ Class: __________

What Is "Sustainable" Agriculture? Public Service Announcement Evaluation

Category/ Expectations	Criteria	Level 1	Level 2	Level 3	Level 4
Knowledge and Understanding ■ Describe the effects of various economic factors on food production and supply ■ Demonstrate an understanding of the effects of different environmental factors and issues on the production and supply of food items	■ Educates the public about sustainability ■ Content in PSA and media release is accurate ■ Content in PSA and media release is thorough				
Thinking and Inquiry ■ Investigate the impact of a variety of political factors on food quality, production and supply ■ Identify current food crises, the factors causing each of them and their impact on the availability and cost of food	■ The effects and impacts of economics, politics and environment on food production and supply ■ Media release examines the reasons for the campaign				
Communication ■ Effectively communicate the results of their inquiries, using a variety of methods and forms	■ The announcement is appropriate for the general public ■ The media release is written to the appropriate audience ■ The message is organized and clearly presented ■ Spelling and grammar ■ Neatly presented				

Name: ______________________ Date: __________ Class: __________

4-8

Issues in Biotechnology—Letter to the Editor

Specific Expectations

- Identify the impact of biotechnology on food production, supply, and safety
- Identify legislation governing pesticide and fertilizer use, food additives, and the labelling of biogenetically engineered foods
- Evaluate print and electronic sources on food and nutrition for bias, accuracy, validity, authority, and relevance
- Record information and key ideas gathered from their research, and document sources accurately, using correct forms of citation
- Effectively communicate the results of their inquiries, using a variety of methods and forms

Biotechnology is the scientific process of altering the genetic make-up of an organism, which changes the inherited traits of the original organism. This process is not a new one, but has been going on for hundreds of years in the form of selective breeding. For more information on biotechnology, visit some of the following web sites:

Canadian Food Inspection Agency, Science Branch, Office of Biotechnology at www.inspection.gc.ca/english/sci/biotech/bioteche.shtml

Council for Biotechnology Information at www.whybiotech.com/

Dieticians of Canada Nutrition Resources at www.dieticians.ca/resources/index.html

Your Task:

Write a letter to your local newspaper stating your concerns about changing agriculture practices such as biotechnology or aquaculture. Be sure when you are researching for your letter that you examine your sources with a critical eye. This has been a controversial topic at times and much of the information presented may be biased.

Letters to the editor are one of the best and easiest ways to get an unfiltered message about a particular issue out to the community. They are your chance to "sound off" to your community about issues in the news. Letters to the editor are generally brief, to the point, and respond to a previously written article or public event. They are so effective because the editorial page is one of the most-read sections of the paper. The address to which to send your letter to the editor usually appears on the editorial page.

When writing a letter to the editor, keep the following points in mind:

- Following your opening sentence, immediately begin to make your case.
- Make one point (or at most two) in your letter. State the point clearly, ideally in the first sentence.
- Make your letter timely. If you are not addressing a specific article, editorial, or recent letter, then try to tie your issue to a recent event.

- When you close the letter to the editor, include a call to action for the general public. This could be calling an MP or MPP, attending a meeting, boycotting a company, or writing a letter to the appropriate people.
- Familiarize yourself with the coverage and editorial position of the paper to which you are writing. Refute or support specific statements, address relevant facts that are have been ignored, but avoid blanket attacks on the media in general or the newspaper in particular.
- Check the letter specifications of the newspaper. Length and format requirements vary from paper to paper. In general, it is better to have a shorter letter than a longer one, as it is more likely to be read (however, you still need to make all of the your points). Keep it short and concise—150–200 words. The paper may shorten your letter to suit its format; the more it has to cut, the less control you have of what gets is printed. Lead with your most important information.
- When you submit your letter to the editor, include your name, address, and daytime telephone number. Your name is needed because anonymous letters are not as credible as those that are signed.
- Look at the letters that appear in your paper. Is a certain type of letter frequently printed?

ISSUES IN BIOTECHNOLOGY—LETTER TO THE EDITOR
Evaluation

Category/ Expectations	Criteria	Level 1	Level 2	Level 3	Level 4
Knowledge and Understanding ■ Identify the impact of biotechnology on food production, supply, and safety ■ Identify legislation governing pesticide and fertilizer use, food additives, and the labelling of biogenetically engineered foods	■ Educates the public about issues in biotechnology ■ Content is accurate and thorough ■ Statistics are provided to support argument				
Thinking and Inquiry ■ Evaluate print and electronic sources on food and nutrition for bias, accuracy, validity, authority, and relevance	■ Present the consequences of not addressing these issues ■ A concise and well organized argument is presented				
Communication ■ Record information and key ideas gathered from their research, and document sources accurately, using correct forms of citation ■ Effectively communicate the results of their inquiries, using a variety of methods and forms	■ Sources are cited ■ The letter is written to the appropriate audience ■ The message is organized and clearly presented ■ Spelling and grammar ■ Neatly presented				
Application ■ Identify the impact of biotechnology on food production, supply, and safety	■ Call for action provides practical and realistic solutions				

Name: ______________________ Date: __________ Class: __________

4-9

Careers in Agriculture

Specific Expectations

- Use a variety of print and electronic sources to find information on employment opportunities in areas relating to food and nutrition sciences, such as health and medicine, hospitality services, agriculture, and food technology and production
- Demonstrate the effective use of data-collection skills and methods, including questionnaires, interviews, and surveys
- Compile information from a variety of primary research sources and secondary sources
- Effectively communicate the results of their inquiries, using a variety of methods and forms

Your task is to investigate a career in agriculture using primary research methods, specifically interviews. Interviews are an excellent method for gathering data. You will be able to ask open-ended questions that will allow you to learn more about your chosen career.

Steps

1. Choose a career in agriculture that you would like to learn more about. Many careers are profiled on www.agriscience.ca/studentguide/e_toc.html.
2. Research your career to prepare appropriate interview questions. Submit your questions to your teacher for approval before starting your interview.
3. Choose and contact a person in your chosen field. Set up a time, date, and location for the interview.
4. You may tape, video, or transcribe the interview. Whatever form it takes, you will submit your interview for evaluation.
5. After completing your interview prepare a one-page reaction to the interview. What were your impressions of the career? What did you learn? Would you consider this career for your future? Compare the results of your interview to the secondary research you conducted prior to composing your interview questions. Identify any similarities and differences.

Name: ______________________ Date: __________ Class: __________

Assessment and Evaluation

Category/ Expectations	Criteria	Level 1	Level 2	Level 3	Level 4
Knowledge and Understanding ■ Use a variety of print and electronic sources to find information on employment opportunities in areas relating to food and nutrition sciences, such as health and medicine, hospitality services, agriculture, and food technology and production	■ Summarizes the results of the interview				
Thinking and Inquiry ■ Compile information from a variety of primary research sources and secondary sources	■ Analyze interview data collected comparing it to secondary research ■ Interprets results of the interview				
Communication ■ Effectively communicate the results of their inquiries, using a variety of methods and forms	■ The written report communicates ideas clearly and concisely				
Application ■ Demonstrate the effective use of data-collection skills and methods, including questionnaires, interviews, and surveys	■ Interview questions are written to gather appropriate data				

Name: ______________________ Date: __________ Class: __________

STUDY GUIDE **4-10**

Trends in Food Preparation and Consumption in Canada

Refer to pages 604–621 to complete the following questions.

Knowledge and Understanding

1. Define the following terms.

Tracking Nutrition Trends 2001 survey	
Canadian Nutrition Facts table	
Functional food	
Nutraceutical	
Phytochemicals	
Antioxidants	
Free radicals	
Omega-3	
Texturized vegetable protein	
Special-purpose food	
Aseptic packages	
Irradiation	
Organic foods	

Thinking and Inquiry

2. Identify five current trends in Canadian society and explain how each will impact the development of new food products and services. Follow the example given.

Name: ______________________ Date: __________ Class: __________

Trend	New Food Products and Services
■ People over 50 is the fastest-growing age group	■ Food industries focus on this group. ■ Create products addressing health concerns.

3. What does the Canadian consumer want when making food choices? List six aspects of food that affect the choices we make.

Communication

4. Complete the following chart by identifying two food products that carry these nutritional claims. You can complete this activity at home, at the grocery store, using grocery store flyers, or in your school's foods lab.

Nutritional Claim	Food Products
■ Cholesterol-free	
■ Low in saturated fat	
■ Source of fibre	
■ Light	
■ Good source of calcium	

After completing the activity above, locate at least three food products that contain the Heart and Stroke Foundation's Health Check logo. List the foods and explain why you think each food received this recommendation.

Food Item	Why Is It Recommended?

5. Explain the role of antioxidants and phytochemicals in the prevention of cancer.

6. For each of the following food products identify how scientific advancements have led to new health benefits. Complete the chart following the example given.

Food Product	Current Research	Impact on Food
■ Eggs	■ Omega-3 (a polyunsaturated fat) reduces the risk of heart disease. ■ Eggs as a functional food improve vision due to antioxidants.	■ Hens are fed special diet of ground flaxseed to produce Omega-3 eggs.
■ Soy-Based Products (foods and drinks)		
■ Whole-Grain Products		
■ Yogurt		
■ Calcium		

7. According to *Foodservice and Hospitality* magazine, breakfast is the food-service industry's fastest-growing phenomenon. How could you prove this statement is true? How would you explain this trend?

8. Explain how supermarkets are attempting to meet the nutritional needs of busy Canadian families and individuals.

9. How have advances in food packaging affected both the nutritional value of food and the quality of the environment?

10. List four new developments in food packaging. For each development explain why it is used.

11. How does organic farming differ from conventional farming techniques? What are some advantages and disadvantages of purchasing and consuming organic foods?

Name: ______________________ Date: __________ Class: __________

4-11

FOOD LAB

Comparing Organic and Non-Organic Foods Lab

Choose a food product that can be purchased in both the organic and regular sections of the grocery store such as hamburgers, pasta, tomato sauce, potato chips, or cookies.

If necessary, prepare the food as directed.

Complete the following chart to compare the organic and non-organic prepared foods.

Name of Food:

Quality	Organic Sample	Non-Organic Sample
Price		
Appearance		
Taste		
Texture		
Smell		
Cost		
Packaging		

FOOD LAB, *continued*

In the chart below, reproduce the ingredients lists of the two foods. Compare the ingredients. How are they similar? How do they differ?

Refer to the packaging and note any nutritional claims made by each product. Which do you prefer? Why?

Organic foods are usually more expensive than their non-organic counterparts. Do you think the organic version of the food is worth the extra cost?

Organic Ingredients	Non-Organic Ingredients

Name: ______________________ Date: __________ Class: __________

4-12

Food Packaging Technology

Specific Expectations

- Identify new developments in food preparation and service
- Use a variety of print and electronic sources and telecommunications tools to investigate and report on the technology behind some of the new food products and trends that will influence eating habits in the future
- Effectively communicate the results of their inquiries, using a variety of methods and forms
- Design, cost, market, produce, and evaluate a food product (e.g., flavoured vinegar, sugared nutmeats, seasonal cookies).

Packaging has been around for as long as there have been human communities. Nature's packaging of foodstuffs such as coconuts, eggs, shellfish, and bananas inspired people to look for ways to store and protect their food and belongings. Prehistoric people used nature for their packaging—leaves, reed baskets, and animal skins. As human communities evolved, so did their packaging. Technology may have changed, and packaging definitely has changed, but ultimately the function of packaging has remained the same:

- To contain liquids, solids, and gases.
- To protect fragile goods.
- To preserve food and prevent spoilage.
- To allow for easy transportation.
- To instruct, inform, and warn the purchaser through labelling.
- To attract the purchaser.

Today's packages also serve a number of new needs. Today's packaging must help to promote and differentiate products from others and be environmentally friendly. Consumers are also looking for convenience, and packaging needs to be easy to handle and dispense.

(**Source**: Careers in a Package, Packaging Careers Council of Canada, www.packagingcareers.org. Retrieved July 6, 2004.)

Brainstorm as many different types of food packaging as you can. For each type of packaging identify examples of foods contained in it.

Choose three of the following types of packaging and research the Internet for information regarding the technology used in the packaging.

- Aseptic packages (also called Tetra Paks™).
- Potato chip bags.
- Recycled glass.
- Polyethylene terephthalate (PET).
- Juice pouches.
- Other type approved by the teacher.

Name: ______________________ Date: __________ Class: __________

FOOD LAB, *continued* **4-12**

Suggested Resources

Food Engineering
www.foodengineeringmag.com/CDA/ArticleInformation/features/BNP__Features__Item/0,6330,118362,00.html
Packaging Today www.packagingtoday.com/
Packaging Digest www.packagingdigest.com/
Packaging Online www.packaging-online.com/paperboardpackaging/

After researching your selected type of packaging, create a visual display to be used by a packaging company trying to promote the use of their technology and packaging. Salespeople could use the display when visiting prospective clients. Your display can be in the form of a pamphlet, booklet, poster, PowerPoint™ display board etc.

Begin designing your display by brainstorming what companies would need to know about your product. Next, locate information about the product. The Internet is likely to be your best source of research, but you may also be able to access professional journals and other research at your public library.

FOOD PACKAGING TECHNOLOGY Evaluation

Category/ Expectations	Criteria	Level 1	Level 2	Level 3	Level 4
Knowledge and Understanding ■ Identify new developments in food preparation and service	■ Educates the customer about the uses and benefits of your packaging ■ Content is accurate and thorough				
Thinking and Inquiry ■ Use a variety of print and electronic sources and telecommunications tools to investigate and report on the technology behind some of the new food products and trends that will influence eating habits in the future	■ Information is presented to customer in a manner that promotes the product, encourages the customer to use it				
Communication ■ Effectively communicate the results of their inquiries, using a variety of methods and forms	■ The message is organized and clearly presented ■ Company contact information is included ■ Spelling and grammar ■ Graphics are used to communicate message				
Application ■ Design, cost, market, produce, and evaluate a food product (e.g., flavoured vinegar, sugared nutmeats, seasonal cookies).	■ Practical applications of the technology are included ■ Samples of products using packaging technology are included				

Unit 4: Test Bank

1. What are food additives?
   a. Chemicals added to food to preserve freshness or enhance colour or flavour
   b. Chemicals added to prevent people from having food allergy reactions
   c. Chemicals added to remove some of the nutrients
   d. All of the above

2. What agency is responsible for the control of food additives in Canada's food supply?
   a. Health Canada
   b. Centre of Science in the Public Interest
   c. Dietitians of Canada
   d. World Health Organization

3. Phenylketonuria (PKU) is a metabolic disorder where:
   a. you are unable to metabolize lactose
   b. you can't eat foods containing aspartame
   c. you must carry an epinephrine injection with you everywhere you go
   d. you will develop a rash, itchiness and hives

4. Caffeine
   a. is a depressant
   b. is an additive that is added to coffee and tea
   c. is a stimulant that occurs naturally in coffee and tea
   d. is safe to consume if during pregnancy

5. Which substance slows down or prevents rancidity in fats and oils and prevents browning when fruits or vegetables are cut and exposed to the air?
   a. Artificial colour
   b. Emulsifier
   c. Antioxidant
   d. Anti-caking agent

6. Functional foods
   a. are sold in medicinal form and not usually associated with foods
   b. have a physiological benefit and reduce the risk of chronic disease
   c. are not normally consumed as part of a regular diet
   d. include chocolate bars, potato chips and ice cream

7. Texturized vegetable protein is
   a. created from dried vegetables
   b. sold as a wet paste
   c. is similar in texture to ground beef
   d. has a strong flavour

8. Yogurt is
a. more popular today than it was in the past.
b. is a photobiotic food.
c. helps to improve the balance of microbes in the human intestinal tract.
d. are more easily digested than milk for most people.
e. all of the above

9. Herbs
a. are the buds, bark, seeds, stem and roots of plants and trees.
b. can provide extra flavour for those trying to reduce their salt consumption.
c. are peppercorns, cumin seeds, cardamom and cinnamon.
d. are only sold fresh.

10. Breakfast as part of the food service industry is
a. one of the slower growing areas.
b. growing by more than 60 percent over the past eight years.
c. always a healthy alternative
d. most often eaten at home and therefore restaurants don't consider it an important part of their business.

11. Which of the following demographic trends have led to significant changes in the way we eat (choose all that apply)
a. decreasing family size
b. more stay at home parents
c. less single-parent homes
d. the fastest growing age group is over 50 years
e. more ethnically diverse population

12. Recent changes to food packaging have included
a. aseptic packages.
b. foil containers for microwavable foods.
c. less reliance on frozen food packaging.
d. packages that serve large groups of people.

13. Bottled water
a. is less popular today than in the past.
b. is more popular today because people feel it is safer than tap water.
c. is more likely to be susceptible to waterborne illness.
d. bottles should be refilled.

14. Farm size is
a. decreasing.
b. increasing along with farm population.
c. increasing but farm population is decreasing.
d. remaining constant.

15. The average age of farmers is
a. increasing. **b.** decreasing. **c.** remaining constant.

16. The government program that is similar to a savings account and allows farmers to deposit money during the good times and withdraw it when times are tough, is called
a. Canadian Farm Income Program.
b. Net Income Stabilization Account.
c. Farmers Saving Program.
d. Canadian Farmers Insurance Program.

17. Match the term on the left with its definition on the right:

____ conventional tillage	**a.** where most of crop residue is left on the surface for the winter
____ low tillage	**b.** substance that provide plants with nutrients
____ pesticides	**c.** most of the residue from the crop is tilled back into the soil
____ fertilizers	**d.** a product used to manage, destroy, attract, and repel unwanted organisms
____ bioengineering	**e.** the science of farming in water
____ aquaculture	**f.** to stop the ripening process
	g. the process of altering the genetic makeup of an organism

18. Farmers determine the best type of fertilizer to use based on which of the following criteria—choose all that apply:
a. climate
b. the type of crop being grown
c. the type of soil
d. the safety of the fertilizer

Communication

19. You are a food scientist working for a food company. Lately, the company has found that consumers are concerned about the amount of additives in packaged foods. Your job is to create an explanation for consumers about the role of additives. Create a newsletter that explains the roles of additives, identifies some typical additives, and lists some products that contain them.

20. Write a letter to the editor of your local newspaper stating your concerns about the current state of agriculture in Canada. You may choose to address your concerns around the shrinking farm population, the urbanization of farm land, agriculture conservation practices, or innovations in agriculture. Be sure that you examine the issues with a critical eye.

Application

21. Based on your knowledge of current trends in the areas of food and nutrition your task is to create a new snack. Complete the following chart detailing your plans for your new snack food.

Characteristics of Your Snack Food	
Snack description and ingredients	
Target Consumer	
What consumer needs are you meeting?	
What competition do you face?	
What types of product testing will you complete prior to producing and marketing your product? Why is this your best route?	
How will you package your snack? Explain why this is your best alternative.	
Price of the snack. How did you establish this price?	
Where will you sell your snack? Why did you decide on this location?	
How will you market/advertise your snack?	

Name: ____________________ Date: __________ Class: __________

4-14

Contemporary Issues in Food

Specific Expectations

- Summarize and interpret articles on food and nutrition found in newspapers, magazines, and selected research literature, as well as on the internet
- Distinguish between key and supporting issues in formulating questions to be researched or problems to be solved
- Differentiate between research evidence and opinion
- Record information and key ideas gathered from their research, and document sources accurately, using correct forms of citation
- Effectively communicate the results of their inquiries, using a variety of methods and forms
- Identify current food crises, the factors causing each of them, and their impact on the availability and costs of food
- Correctly uses the terminology of food and nutrition sciences

Choose a present-day issue related to food and nutrition such as mad cow disease, water contamination, genetically modified foods, corporate farming, food irradiation, antibiotic use in farming, cod fishing on the East Coast, zebra mussels, organic foods, pesticide use, or aquaculture. Research the issue and then write a 500 - 750 word position paper. The position paper should both define and defend your position. Position papers present one side of a controversial issue and try Your arguments must be supported by logic, facts, statistics, and expert opinion. Remember to cite all sources using APA referencing style and in-text citations.

CULMINATING ACTIVITY, *continued*

Assessment and Evaluation

Category/ Expectations	Criteria	Level 1	Level 2	Level 3	Level 4
Knowledge and Understanding ■ Identify current food crises, the factors causing each of them, and their impact on the availability and costs of food ■ Correctly uses the terminology of food and nutrition sciences	■ Accuracy of information ■ Facts, statistics, expert opinion are used to support position				
Thinking and Inquiry ■ Distinguish between key and supporting issues in formulating questions to be researched or problems to be solved ■ Differentiate between research evidence and opinion	■ Present an effective number of arguments to support position ■ Clarity of evaluation and analysis				
Communication ■ Summarize and interpret articles on food and nutrition found in newspapers, magazines, and selected research literature, as well as on the internet ■ Effectively communicate the results of their inquiries, using a variety of methods and forms	■ Clearly present an effective argument ■ Introduction clearly states position on issue ■ Conclusion summaries main ideas presented in paper ■ Smooth flow of ideas ■ Spelling, grammar and style				
Application ■ Record information and any ideas gathered from their research, and document sources accurately, using correct terms and citations	■ Documents all sources using APA referencing style ■ Uses in-text citations where appropriate				

Creating a New Food Product

Course Culminating Activity

Phase One: Identify the Product

The Culminating Activity for this course is divided into four phases. For this task you will work as part of a design and production team to create and market a new food product. The product must meet an identified need in the marketplace, and it must have significant nutritional value.

Each phase of the Culminating Activity will be completed at the end of the appropriate unit and evaluated at that time. Each phase will lead into the next phase so it is important that you complete each phase on time.

In **Phase One** your task is to identify the type of product your group would like to create. Your team will base their initial planning on the knowledge that you have gained in Unit One of this course. You should also take some time to research current media (e.g., magazines, newspapers, television shows) to identify what is in the news and what issues about nutrition currently concern the public.

Once you have decided on the product you will create, you will then need to identify its key nutrients and their function or value. Your team will also determine how your product will fulfill a need felt in the marketplace.

Food for Today, First Canadian Edition, References

Chapter 11 Nutrient Wise
Chapter 14 Diet, Lifestyle, and Health

Expectations Met by Phase One

- Design, cost, market, produce, and evaluate a food product (e.g., flavoured vinegar, sugared nutmeats, seasonal cookies).
- Explain the relationship among lifestyle, food choices, and nutrition-related illnesses and diseases (e.g., cardiovascular disease, anorexia nervosa, tooth decay, osteoporosis).
- Correctly use the terminology of food and nutrition sciences (e.g., *nutrient deficiencies, food security, vegetarianism, cuisine, agribusiness, gluten development*).
- Effectively communicate the results of their inquiries, using a variety of methods and forms (e.g., graphs, charts, diagrams, oral presentations, written reports, videos).
- Summarize and interpret articles on food and nutrition found in newspapers, magazines, and selected research literature, as well as on the Internet
- Identify new developments in food preparation and service (e.g., types of restaurant service, ways of presenting foods, styles of kitchens in the home, kitchen appliances).

Note: In Phase Two of the project you will conduct primary research to determine if the product that you are interested in creating is likely to be a success. You will need to see if others in your selected market would be interested in your project. If they are not interested, you will need to make revisions to Phase One.

Name: ______________________ Date: __________ Class: __________

Creating a New Food Product
Phase One: Identify the Product

Names of Team Members :

1. ______________________

2. ______________________

3. ______________________

4. ______________________

1. Identify your target market. To whom are you directing your product? (e.g., young children, teenagers, parents, athletes, older adults)

2. Provide a brief summary of the research you conducted. What types of nutritional concerns were voiced at this time? What is your target market concerned about? Include a brief list of your research sources.

3. Brainstorm a list of products that your group could create that might interest your target audience. Remember that brainstorming means listing as many ideas as you can. No evaluating at this time!

Name: ____________________ Date: __________ Class: __________

4. Complete the following chart, evaluating each of your ideas. Your evaluation should address the relationship between food choices and nutrition-related conditions and diseases.

Idea	This Is a Good Idea Because...	Problem Might Be...

5. We have decided to create ____________________ as our product because __________

____

____

____

6. Based on your knowledge of nutrition, identify the nutrients you intend to be part of your food product. For example, if you have decided to create a breakfast cereal, it most likely would contain carbohydrates, vitamin B_1, B_2, B_3, folic acid and iron. For each nutrient, identify its function or role in a healthy diet.

Name: ______________________ Date: __________ Class: __________

Nutrient	Function/Role in a Healthy Diet

Name: ______________________ Date: __________ Class: __________

Creating a New Food Product
Phase One: Assessment and Evaluation

Category	Level 1	Level 2	Level 3	Level 4
Knowledge and Understanding ■ Correctly use terminology of food and nutrition sciences. ■ Identify new developments in food preparation and service (e.g., types of restaurant service, ways of presenting foods, styles of kitchens in the home, kitchen appliances).				
Thinking and Inquiry ■ Summarize and interpret articles on food and nutrition found in newspapers, magazines, and selected research literature, as well as on the internet. ■ Explain the relationship among lifestyle, food choices, and nutrition-related illnesses and diseases (e.g., cardiovascular disease, anorexia nervosa, tooth decay, osteoporosis).				
Communication ■ Effectively communicate results of inquiries, using a variety of methods and forms (e.g., graphs, charts, diagrams, oral presentations, written reports, videos).				
Application ■ Design, cost, market, produce, and evaluate a food product (e.g., flavoured vinegar, sugared nutmeats, seasonal cookies).				

Name: ______________________________ Date: __________ Class: __________

Creating a New Food Product

Course Culminating Activity

Phase Two: Market Research

During **Phase Two** of the project you and your team will conduct primary research to determine the needs of the marketplace and how those needs can best be addressed. Based on your initial planning in Phase One, you now must determine whether the product you are interested in creating has a good chance of being successful. You need to find out if others in your selected market would be interested in your product.

The Process:

Your team will begin this phase by creating a questionnaire of at least 15 questions. It should contain both background and content questions. The background questions will describe your proposed product. . Your content questions will relate to how your product will meet the needs of your target audience. Will people buy it? What price will they pay? What type of packaging will work best? What will be the best way to advertise and promote it?

Be sure to proofread your questionnaire carefully. Have your teacher approve it before you distribute it. Distribute your survey to a minimum of 20 people who fit your target audience.

After distributing your survey, tally your results and analyze the results of your survey. Each question should be accompanied by a graph (e.g., bar, pie chart, line graph) that displays your results.

After completing your market research and analysis, write your recommendations for your new food product. Include specific information based on the questions that you asked in your questionnaire. Decide how best to present this information (e.g., poster, booklet, computer-generated presentation).

Food for Today, First Canadian Edition, References

- **Chapter 2**, Why People Eat the Foods They Do
- **Chapter 4**, Food Marketing
- **Chapter 11**, Nutrient Wise
- **Chapter 13**, Personal Eating Habits
- **Chapter 14**, Diet, Lifestyle, and Health
- **Chapter 28**, Nutritional Status of Canadians

Expectations Met by Phase Two

- Identify psychological and emotional factors that affect eating habits (e.g., eating to relieve tension or boredom, deriving comfort from food).
- Describe economic factors that have an impact on the food choices of individuals and families.
- Identify the ways in which physical factors influence food choices (e.g., geographical location, regional growing seasons, availability of food markets, home storage capacity).
- Identify the factors that affect personal food choices throughout the life cycle (e.g., age, health, school and/or work schedules, lifestyle, level of physical activity, lactation, special dietary needs).

Name: ______________________ Date: __________ Class: __________

- Plan, conduct, and summarize the results of an investigation into the availability of food products suitable for various stages of the life cycle (e.g., single-serving products, baby food, fat-reduced food).
- Demonstrate the effective use of data-collection skills and methods, including questionnaires, interviews, and surveys.
- Effectively communicate the results of their inquiries, using a variety of methods and forms (e.g., graphs, charts, diagrams, oral presentations, written reports, videos).

Creating a New Food Product
Phase Two: Assessment and Evaluation

Category	Level 1	Level 2	Level 3	Level 4
Knowledge and Understanding ■ Identify appropriate target audience for survey. ■ Plan and design questionnaire that allows researchers to obtain needed information.				
Thinking and Inquiry ■ Create questions that iden-tify the various factors that impact on food choices (i.e., stage of lifecycle, psychological, emotional, physical, economic, availability of food). ■ Perform a thorough analysis of questionnaire data.				
Communication ■ Effectively communicate results of survey and inquiries using graphs, charts, written reports. ■ Plan, conduct, and summarize the results of an investigation into the availability of food products suitable for various stages of the life cycle (e.g., single-serving products, baby food, fat-reduced food).				
Application ■ Demonstrate effective use of data collection skills and methods, including questionnaires, interviews, and surveys.				

Name: ______________________ Date: __________ Class: __________

Creating a New Food Product

Course Culminating Activity

Phase Three: Designing the Product

During **Phase Three** you will take into account the data collected during Phase Two and begin to create your product. You will conduct a test run and make any revisions necessary.

The Process

Review the data collected in Phase Two. Use this information to create your product.
Next, find or create a recipe and make adjustments to your recipe as necessary. You may have to prepare a few (or more) different samples before you feel confident that you have it right. Ask a number of people to sample your product and make suggestions. Keep track of all suggestions using the evaluation chart provided. Be sure to give credit to the source of your recipe.

One of your main goals is to produce a product without damaging the Earth or harming your employees. Identify the origin of the ingredients you use to make your product and examine any ethical issues related to the manufacture of your product. How will you address these issues? You may present this information in the form of a written report or in chart form.

Recipe Evaluation Chart

Name of Product:

Sampler's Name:

Sample #	Appearance	Texture	Description of Flavour(s)	Suggestions for improvement	Ranking
1					
2					
3					
4					

Name: ______________________________ Date: __________ Class: __________

***Food for Today, First Canadian Edition*, References**

- **Chapter 22**, Our Aboriginal Food Heritage
- **Chapter 23**, Canada's Regional Foods
- **Chapter 24**, Canadian Food Supply and Production
- **Chapter 26**, Staple Foods of the World
- **Chapter 30**, World Cuisines
- **Chapter 32**, Food Security and Hunger

Expectations Met by Phase Three

- Plan menus for, select, and prepare foods, taking into consideration economic, geographical, and seasonal factors that affect the availability of ingredients.
- Investigate the impact of a variety of political factors on food quality, production, and supply (e.g., international food policies, national and provincial food policies, food marketing boards), and present the results of their investigation.
- Demonstrate an understanding of the effects of different environmental factors and issues on the production and supply of food items (e.g., energy and resources required to produce various foods; use of pesticides, fertilizers, food additives, and irradiation).
- Effectively communicate the results of their inquiries, using a variety of methods and forms (e.g., graphs, charts, diagrams, oral presentations, written reports, videos).

Name: ____________________ Date: __________ Class: __________

Creating a New Food Product
Phase Three: Assessment and Evaluation

Category/Expectations	Level 1	Level 2	Level 3	Level 4
Knowledge and Understanding ■ Demonstrate an understanding of the effects of different environmental factors and issues on the production and supply of food items (e.g., energy and resources required to produce various foods; use of pesticides, fertilizers, food additives, and irradiation).				
Thinking and Inquiry ■ Investigate the impact of a variety of poitical factors on food quality, production, and supply (e.g., international food policies, national and provincial food policies, food marketing boards), and present the results of investigation.				
Communication ■ Effectively communicate results of inquiries, using a variety of methods and forms (e.g., graphs, charts, diagrams, oral presentations, written reports, videos).				
Application ■ Plan menus for, select, and prepare foods, taking into consideration economic, geographical, and seasonal factors that affect the availability of ingredients.				

Name: ______________________________ Date: __________ Class: __________

Creating a New Food Product

Course Culminating Activity

Phase Four: Production and Marketing

In the final stage of this process your team will produce and market the final product. You will design your packaging, distribute your product, and evaluate the success of your project.

The Process

Based on the results of Phase Three, in **Phase Four** you and your team will produce the final product. Remember that food is a sensual experience—the senses must be engaged. Food that doesn't look good will not sell. Make sure that your production process is safe and environmentally friendly.

You and your team will also need to design and create the packaging for your product. Examine new and innovative ways of packaging. How can you best address concerns about shipping, safety, convenience, and storage?

Now develop a marketing plan for your product. How will you advertise your product? Which media will be used and why? Identify all of the factors that go into determining the cost to produce your product. How much will it cost to make? How much will the consumer pay?

Market and sell your product. This may mean selling it within your school or local community.

Evaluate your team's success. What went well? What challenges did you and your team encounter? How did you address these challenges? Did you capture your market's attention?

Food for Today, First Canadian Edition, References

- **Chapter 29,** Trends in Food Preparation and Consumption

Expectations Met by Phase Four

- Identify new developments in food preparation and service (e.g., types of restaurant service, ways of presenting foods, styles of kitchens in the home, kitchen appliances).
- Design, cost, market, produce, and evaluate a food product (e.g., flavoured vinegar, sugared nutmeats, seasonal cookies)
- Demonstrate the effective use of data-collection skills and methods, including questionnaires, interviews, and surveys.
- Effectively communicate the results of their inquiries, using a variety of methods and forms(e.g., graphs, charts, diagrams, oral presentations, written reports, videos).

Name: ______________________ Date: __________ Class: __________

Creating a New Food Product
Phase Four: Assessment and Evaluation

Category	Level 1	Level 2	Level 3	Level 4
Knowledge and Understanding ■ Identify new developments in food preparation and service (e.g., types of restaurant service, ways of presenting foods, styles of kitchens in the home, kitchen appliances).				
Thinking and Inquiry ■ Describe economic factors that have an impact on the food choices of individuals and families.				
Communication ■ Effectively communicate results of inquiries, using a variety of methods and forms (e.g., graphs, charts, diagrams, oral presentations, written reports, videos).				
Application ■ Design, cost, market, produce, and evaluate a food product (e.g., flavoured vinegar, sugared nutmeats, seasonal cookies).				

Food and Nutrition Sciences (HFA4M)
SAFETY FIRST APPENDIX

Since the prerequisite for *Food and Nutrition Sciences* (HFA4M) is, "Any university, university/college, or college preparation course in social sciences and humanities, English or Canadian and world studies," it is likely that many students taking the course will not have received the training necessary to work in a family studies classroom in a safe and healthy manner. While there are no expectations in the curriculum document that refer specifically to health and safety in the family studies classroom, attention to safety is implicit throughout. The curriculum policy document for *Social Sciences and Humanities, Grade 11 and 12* (2000) states:

> In family studies courses, teachers must take particular care to ensure that safety requirements are met and safety procedures followed when students are involved in practical activities. Students must be made aware of any health or safety hazards that might be connected with the activities in which they are engaged and must be coached in the proper use of safety equipment, such as fire extinguishers. Schools must provide pre-placement health and safety instruction for students in work experience and cooperative education programs. Employers are expected to provide placement-specific health and safety training as part of a student's learning plan. (p. 141)

The course description for HFA4M lists the following expectations that require an understanding and application of health and safety requirements in the family studies lab environment:

- Plan menus for, select, and prepare foods, taking into consideration economic, geographical, and seasonal factors that affect the availability of ingredients.
- Plan a menu for, select, and prepare foods that would meet selected dietary needs during the stages of life.
- Use available resources, including computer technology, both to plan a menu consisting of foods that will maintain good health, and to select and prepare those foods.
- Demonstrate how to use equipment correctly to prepare and store foods for maximum nutrient retention (e.g., steamer, pressure cooker, freezer).
- Design, cost, market, produce, and evaluate a food product (e.g., flavoured vinegar, sugared nutmeats, seasonal cookies).
- Demonstrate an understanding of the scientific principles of a variety of types of food preparation (e.g., starch cookery, gluten development, protein cookery).
- Plan, prepare, and serve (using available ingredients and technology) specific foods prepared in the style of a variety of ethnic and/or Native cuisines, and draw comparisons among them.
- Prepare a menu using some new food products or recipes, and evaluate the results.

Food and Nutrition Sciences (HFA4M) offers opportunities for practical application of knowledge gained throughout the course.

Potential Hazards in the Family Studies Kitchen

Most family studies kitchens are set up to resemble a home kitchen environment. Therefore, hazards that are present in the home may also be present in the family studies kitchen. Stoves, knives, small equipment, electrical appliances, kitchen cabinets, and drawers all hold the potential for injury. Some household hazards such as accidental ingestion of a poisonous cleanser, may not be present, as many boards prohibit the use of such products in schools. However, there are many opportunities for accidents to occur in the kitchen, and virtually all equipment used has the potential to contribute to an accident. Personal safety is a primary concern in the kitchen and must be addressed before students are allowed to cook. All students must be made aware of the potential hazards and what to do in case of an accident. It is important not only that students not be made anxious about working in the kitchen, but also that they understand that it is possible to prepare food in a safe manner. It should be stressed that accidents in the food lab can happen but are rare.

Since students are preparing and consuming food in the family studies kitchen, they must be aware of the potential for food-borne illnesses and how to prevent these. Again, basic rules and their consistent application will ensure that the food prepared and eaten is safe. Media attention about food-borne illnesses has raised the awareness of the general public. Students may need to be reassured that the preparation of healthy food is possible by following the basic procedures they have learned in class.

Safety is always of primary importance in a foods lab situation. Hazards can be divided into two types: physical and food safety.

Physical Hazards

- Cuts.
- Burns.
- Electrical shock.
- Poisoning.
- Choking.
- Slips and falls.
- Fire.

Biological Hazards

- Bacteria.
- Moulds.
- Yeasts.
- Viruses.
- Fungi.
- Allergic reactions to food.

Chemical Hazards

- Chemical substances.
- Cleaning Agents.
- Pesticides.
- Toxic materials.

Procedures for the Safe Use of Equipment in the Family Studies Kitchen

Safety is an integral part of the family studies program. The physical appearance and organization of the lab should emphasize safety. All equipment should be maintained on a regular basis to ensure a safe working environment for all students and staff. Hang safety posters and other types of reminders throughout the classroom.

The following procedures are applicable to most family studies food labs and can be adjusted to classroom environments. Discuss all procedures with students before using any equipment.

1. General Responsibility

The following suggestions will ensure that students work efficiently and safely.

- Be familiar with the location and use of safety equipment.
- Follow safety rules at all times; always follow the teacher's instructions; work
- Work efficiently, quietly and carefully.
- Share responsibilities and work with others.
- Keep work surfaces orderly; arrange utensils conveniently (crowding the work space causes confusion, spills and accidents); wipe up all spills immediately.
- Practise good personal hygiene in the kitchen area; wash hands with warm water and liquid soap before working with food.
- Wear shoes in the family studies room at all times.
- Keep floor free of grease and water.
- Refrain from running in the family studies room.
- Use caution when reaching over or working beside an appliance that is in use.
- Gather up broken glass immediately; put glass in a separate container beside the garbage pail; label as broken glass.
- Report all accidents, no matter how minor, to the teacher.
- Take care when handling recently cut tops of cans.
- Remove loose fitting clothing, or secure in some way, especially sleeves.
- Ask the teacher if you do not understand the safe procedure for using any electrical appliance or any other piece of equipment in the lab.

2. Safe Use of Knives

- Place knives in drawer with cutting edge down.
- Be sure the knife handle is to the front of the drawer.
- Always use a cutting board.
- Choose the proper size and type of knife for the job.
- Always cut away from the body.
- Wash knives one at a time, not with other tools, and put them away as soon as you are finished.
- Wipe knives by moving the cloth from dull edge to the sharp edge, from base to tip.
- Hand a knife to another person with the handle facing that person; a knife or any sharp tool should never be tossed or slid.
- Use a knife only for its intended purpose, not as a screwdriver, hammer, or can opener.
- Keep knives sharp; dull knives slip more easily than sharp ones.

3. Cookware

- Use cookware that is compatible with the size of the heating unit.
- Never fill cookware more than two-thirds full to minimize the chance of slopping or spilling that may cause burns.
- Avoid steam burns by opening lids away from yourself.
- Keep handles of cookware turned inward on the stove top.
- Always use oven mitts or pot holders on hot items—not aprons, dish towels, or moist cloths.
- Put out grease fires by covering the pot with a lid or using baking soda or a fire extinguisher designed for grease fires.
- Stir hot foods with a wooden or heatproof plastic spoon.

- Do not reach over boiling or steaming liquids.

4. Microwave Ovens

- Do not use metal containers or dishes with metallic trim in the microwave.
- Remove metal twist ties and metal covers or plastic storage wrap before cooking or defrosting.
- Do not microwave paper towels or cloths that contain synthetic fibre.
- Use oven mitts or pot holders when handling hot dishes.
- Do not boil eggs in their shells.
- Do not operate an empty microwave.
- Pierce all foods with nonporous skins before cooking (e.g., potatoes).
- Do not overcook foods, which can cause dehydration and may lead to fire.
- Use only plastic wraps and containers intended for microwave use.

5. Appliances

- Keep electrical appliances and their cords away from water.
- Grasp plug (not cord) when removing from outlet.
- Turn off all electrical appliances when finished using them.
- Always dry hands before plugging or unplugging an electrical appliance.
- Disconnect electric appliance from the outlet, then from the appliance (if removeable)
- Do not use frayed, cracked, or torn electrical cords. Report these to the teacher for repair.
- Keep surfaces free of grease, particularly around the oven and stove top.
- Keep clothing and cloths away from the stove top.
- Do not store flammable objects near the stove.
- Do not overload electrical outlets.

Procedures to Follow in the Event of an Injury

For specific instructions regarding the reporting of injuries, refer to your school's procedures. School boards and schools will vary in the procedures they use; however, the basic procedure is to:

- Call the office for assistance.
- Have a designated, trained individual(s) administer first aid treatment.
- Obtain or recommend medical help
- File a written report with the office.

A fully supplied first aid kit must be available in the family studies room in a prominent location. Consult with your principal to ensure that it contains the supplies recommended by the Board.

The maintenance of safety equipment in the school is the responsibility of the principal; however, teachers should ensure that fire extinguishers are checked regularly and the equipment is correctly located in the classroom.

Letter of Permission to Parents/Guardians

School name ____

Address ____

Date ____

To: The Parents/Guardian of ____________________________,

This semester/year ________________ is taking the family studies course, *Food and Nutrition Sciences* HFA4M as part of his/her Grade 12 studies. We are pleased to be able to provide students with opportunities for hands-on activities that develop their skills and understanding of course material. In these activities students will use machines and equipment with the potential to cause injury. The safety of our students is extremely important to us and we at _______________ school are proud of our safety record in the family studies department.

All students will complete a series of activities concerning safety in the foods classroom before being allowed to work in the foods lab. Students enrolled in *Food and Nutrition Sciences* will learn about safe food-handling practices as well as the correct and safe use of all equipment in the foods lab.

Our aim is to provide ________________ with a safe and enjoyable practical experience that will enhance his/her learning. All students will sign a safety contract that outlines the safety rules and appropriate behaviour in lab situations. Please review this contract and sign in the appropriate place. If you have any questions please do not hesitate to call me at ____________________.

Yours truly,

Family Studies Teacher

SAFETY CONTRACT

As a student enrolled in *Food and Nutrition Sciences, HFA4M*

at ____

(*school name*)

I understand the classroom safety instructions given to me and realize that I have the responsibility to prevent accidents in the classroom.

______________________________ ______________

(*student's signature*) (*date*)

______________________________ ______________

(*parent/caregiver's signature*) (*date*)

______________________________ ______________

(*teacher's signature*) (*date*)

Food Allergies/Considerations

It is extremely important to discover if any students in your class have allergies or intolerances to certain foods and the degree of reaction to those foods these students may suffer. Students with severe or potentially fatal allergies are usually proactive and may carry an Epi-pen™ in case of anaphylactic shock. However, there may be students with less severe reactions who will not be as forthcoming but must also be identified. Take care to ensure that the kitchen does not pose a threat to students with food allergies. If the room is shared with other teachers, they must be made aware of the need to prohibit certain foods.

Consideration may also be given to students who for religious, cultural, or ethical reasons do not eat or handle particular foods.

Have all students with allergies/food considerations complete the form below. Retain the form for the duration of the course.

Student Recording Sheet

Food	Reason (e.g., allergy or sensitivity)	Degree of Reaction	Treatment(s)

Foods Lab Completion Checklist ______________________

At the end of each foods lab the assigned person must complete this checklist and attach it to the foods lab report.

Criteria	Yes	No
Oven is turned off; all stove burners are off.		
All equipment and utensils are washed in hot, soapy water		
All dishes are clean, dried, and put away.		
Knives are returned clean and dry to the knife drawer/container.		
The sink is free of food particles and is clean and dry.		
Dish racks, drainers, and dishpans are washed, dried, and stored under the sink.		
Dish soap and hand soap are stored under the sink.		
Dishtowels, dishcloths, sponges, and aprons are in the laundry basket.		
Any leftover food is stored correctly.		
Tables and placemats are wiped clean and dried.		
All work surfaces are free of food, wiped, and dried.		
Other task as assigned by the teacher completed.		
Floor has been swept.		

Notes to Teacher for Safety Diagnostic Test

Set up one or two kitchens with a series of potential hazards, for example:

- Several appliances plugged into an extension cord
- Appliance cord draped over the sink
- Knives in the sink
- Cleaning products in the cupboard next to food products
- Dishtowel hanging over the oven door
- Oven gloves on the burner
- Pan on incorrect size burner
- Pan handles sticking out
- A spill of some kind on the floor
- 'Meat' (could be a picture) left out on the counter
- Bugs (plastic) on the counter
- Cupboard door open
- Drawer left open

Students can observe the kitchen from a pre-marked distance to record the problems on their test sheets. You may want to allow only one group at a time to do this, depending on the numbers in your class.

Name: ______________________ Date: __________ Class: __________

Practical Safety Hazards Diagnostic Test

This test is a final evaluation of your work on kitchen safety and hygiene. In order to work in the food labs you must achieve a grade of 80% or higher.

Part A—15 marks

Identification of Hazards in the Kitchen

A kitchen has been set up with a series of potential hazards. Identify all the hazards and suggest the correct procedure to avoid an accident or health risk. ($^{1}/_{2}$ mark per hazard, 1 mark for correct procedure)

HAZARD	CORRECT PROCEDURE

Part B—48 marks

Short Answers

Answer the following questions on a separate sheet of paper:

1. **a.** Describe the correct hand washing procedure in detail. (5 marks)
   b. Explain the importance of hand washing in preventing food-borne illness. (2 marks)
   c. Give an example of a situation where improper hand washing could result in illness. (1 mark)

2. A student is cooking apple fritters using a pan of deep fat. You hear a scream and see that the oil is on fire and the student has burnt his/her hand. List five steps you would take (in the correct order) to deal with the situation. (5 marks)

3. Your father has been grocery shopping and asks for your help with storing the groceries. He has purchased the following items: flour, salt, sugar, whole wheat bread, frozen orange juice, tofu, fresh fish, apples, oranges, potatoes, lettuce, carrots, onions, ice cream and frozen corn.
   a. List the foods you would store first and why. (1 mark)
   b. Group the foods into the three main storage areas (3 marks)
   c. State the correct temperature range for each of the three storage areas, and two (2) storage tips for each area. (9 marks)

4. a) State five personal hygiene practices that should be used when working in the kitchen. For each practice explain why it is important.
   (5 marks practises + 5 marks explanation = 10 marks)
   b) Pick one of these practices and explain what could happen if you failed to observe it. (2 marks)

5. If you were preparing grilled chicken for supper, how would you avoid cross-contamination? (2 marks)

6. You have invited some friends over for a barbecue. You have decided to serve grilled hamburgers. You prepare the burgers, put them on a plate and carry them outside. State three procedures you need to practice to help ensure that the food you serve is safe. (3 marks)

7. List the order in which dirty dishes should be washed and explain why it is important that this order be followed. (5 marks)

Name: ______________________ Date: __________ Class: __________

Student Worksheets

Name: ______________________ Date: __________ Class: __________

W-1

DIAGNOSTIC TEST

Getting Ready to Cook

This test is for diagnostic purposes only. Your teacher will review your answers to determine at what level to start the health and safety instruction for this course. Don't worry if you don't know the answers to some of the questions. We will cover the information in the next few days in class.

Read the statement carefully. If the statement is true write T on the line. If the statement is false write F on the line.

1. You cannot get food poisoning in the family studies kitchen at school. __________

2. Eggs are a potential source of salmonella bacteria. __________

3. Hamburgers must be cooked to 74°C in the centre. __________

4. It is OK to defrost frozen chicken on the kitchen counter. __________

5. When purchasing groceries buy perishables (e.g., milk, butter, meat) last. __________

6. It is safe to leave your kettle and toaster plugged in all day. __________

7. The best place to store cleaning products is under the sink. __________

8. Potatoes and onions should be stored under the sink. __________

9. It is fine to use a folded dishtowel to remove a hot dish from the oven. __________

10. Burns should be treated with butter. __________

11. There isn't any equipment in this kitchen that could harm me. __________

12. Hands should be washed only at the start of the foods lab. __________

13. When removing a pot lid, tilt the cover away from your face and body. __________

14. Use water to put out a grease fire. __________

15. If you smell gas, turn off the oven and stove controls, wait one minute, and turn on again. __________

16. Always close cabinet doors and drawers. __________

17. Soak knives in hot, soapy water to ensure that they are cleaned thoroughly. __________

18. Never use metal cookware or aluminum foil in the microwave. __________

19. To unplug an appliance, pull the cord. __________

20. Dishes should not be left to air dry. A dish towel is the most sanitary way to dry dishes. __________

21. List five safety rules to follow when working in the foods lab.

____

____

____

____

____

22. Read the case study below and list the health and safety errors that Preeti made in her food preparation. Give suggestions to correct her mistakes so that the dinner would be prepared in a safe manner and would be safe for her family to eat.

Preeti was making a chicken stir-fry for her family supper. She rushed into the kitchen. The chicken had been defrosting on the counter for three hours but was still partly frozen. Her parents expected dinner in just over a half-hour so Preeti decided to slice the chicken, add some marinade and use it, as it would defrost during cooking.

Preeti took the vegetables from the fridge and, as they looked clean, cut them into neat pieces for her stir-fry. To save time and dishes, she used the same cutting board and knife that she had used for the chicken. Time was running out so Preeti took the rice out of the cupboard under the sink and put some in a pot of boiling water to cook.

She had just started to cook the chicken in the wok when the phone rang. When she returned from the phone the chicken was a little brown and the oil had started to burn. Preeti grabbed the dishtowel and a fork and removed the chicken from the pan. She tipped the hot oil down the sink and ran some water in the pan to clean it. She stir-fried the vegetables quickly, added the chicken, and some of the marinade the chicken had been sitting in. She served the family dinner in record time!

W-1

DIAGNOSTIC TEST—GETTING READY TO COOK, *continued*

Health and Safety Error	Correct Procedure to Follow

Name: ______________________ Date: __________ Class: __________

STUDY GUIDE—SAFETY

W-2

Preventing Kitchen Accidents

Use pages 71–95 of *Food for Today, First Canadian Edition*, to answer the following questions.

A Hazard-Free Kitchen

1. List six general guidelines that are vital to your safety in the kitchen.
   - ______________________
   - ______________________
   - ______________________
   - ______________________
   - ______________________
   - ______________________

2. Complete the following chart, identifying the kitchen hazard and how it can be corrected. Follow the example given.

Kitchen Hazard	Correct Procedure
Preventing Falls	
1. Spills on floor.	1. Wipes up spills promptly
2. ____________	2. ____________
3. ____________	3. ____________
4. ____________	4. ____________
Preventing Cuts	
1. ____________	1. ____________
2. ____________	2. ____________
3. ____________	3. ____________
4. ____________	4. ____________
5. ____________	5. ____________
Using Electricity Safely	
1. ____________	1. ____________
2. ____________	2. ____________
3. ____________	3. ____________
4. ____________	4. ____________

Name: ______________________ Date: __________ Class: __________

W-2

STUDY GUIDE—SAFETY—PREVENTING KITCHEN ACCIDENTS, *continued*

Kitchen Hazard	Correct Procedure
Hazardous Chemicals	
1. ______	1. ______
2. ______	2. ______
3. ______	3. ______
4. ______	4. ______
Stove and Microwave Accidents	
1. ______	1. ______
2. ______	2. ______
3. ______	3. ______
4. ______	4. ______
5. ______	5. ______

3. How should you put out a fire on a stove top or in an electric skillet?

4. How should you handle a fire in an appliance such as an oven, microwave, or toaster oven?

5. List four safety precautions to follow when having young children participate in kitchen activities.

- ______
- ______
- ______
- ______

6. Certain accommodations may be required to ensure kitchen safety for a family member who has a physical challenge. How can you determine what types of changes are needed?

STUDY GUIDE—SAFETY—PREVENTING KITCHEN ACCIDENTS, *continued*

W-2

7. List five things that you can do if an accident happens in the kitchen.
   - ______
   - ______
   - ______
   - ______
   - ______

Keeping Food Safe

8. Match the type of bacteria on the left with its description on the right.

Type of Bacteria	Where Bacteria is Found
a. E. coli	____ raw or undercooked foods, such as poultry, eggs, meat, unpasteurized milk.
b. salmonella	____ on human skin, in nose, and throat—spread by improper food handling.
c. listeria monocytogenes	____ contaminated water, raw or rare ground beef, unpasteurized milk, or apple juice.
d. clostridium perfringens	____ contaminated soil and water, meat and dairy products, ready-to-eat foods such as hot dogs and luncheon meats.
e. staphylococcus aureus	____ improperly processed canned foods, garlic in oil, vacuum-packed or tightly wrapped foods.
f. campylobacter jejuni	____ environments where there is little or no oxygen; spores can survive cooking, most common in cafeterias.
g. clostridium botulinum	____ contaminated water, unpasteurized milk, or under-cooked meat or poultry.

9. What is cross-contamination and how can it be prevented?

10. List and explain the four simple steps to reduce the risk of food borne illness.
    - ______
    - ______
    - ______
    - ______

11. Explain the relationship between food temperature and food safety.

12. List and briefly explain the five environmental conditions that can cause or speed food spoilage.

13. What are some signs that indicate that food has spoiled?

14. Define the term "shelf-stable." How do storage requirements of shelf-stable foods change after the package has been opened?

15. Power outages can be very dangerous for food. What should you do with frozen foods, if there is a power outage? Food kept in a refrigerator? Besides using time as a guideline to determine what to keep and what to dispose of, what else can you do?

"Rules to Keep Fridge Clean and Safe"

The Hamilton Spectator

April 16, 2004

How to tell when it's time to clean out the fridge? When you shake the cream carton but it doesn't swish?

When it would take a DNA test to confirm the origins of the smelly grey stuff at the back of the shelf?

Or is it when the green beans, blanketed in blue velvet, begin to float in the swill at the bottom of the crisper?

There is no scarier place than a dirty fridge. Even the tidiest of housekeepers has at least one refrigerator horror story. …

Food scientists say most people don't take refrigerator hygiene as seriously as they should.

Health Canada estimates about two million cases of foodborne illnesses occur each year. And …the home kitchen is a major source of contamination. A recent survey conducted by the Irish Agriculture and Food Development Authority found patchy food safety practices in many of the 1000 homes the team visited. For instance: the food poisoning pathogen staphylococcus was found in 40 percent of fridges. The more deadly pathogen listeria was found in 6 percent of fridges.

Raw foods, from meat, fish and poultry to cheeses – even fruits and vegetables – often contain microbes such as

E. coli, staphylococcus aureus, salmonella and clostridium botulinum that can cause food poisoning is allowed to multiply. There's mould and mildew, too. The only way to slow their growth is to keep the foods at temperatures at or below 4C (39F) or to throw food put before it gets too old.

Retired MacDonald College food microbiologist Edmund Idziak says many fridges are kept at 7C (45F).

Idziak says most pathogens are killed in cooking. But there's always a danger they will not be heated thoroughly, or that they will come in contact with other contaminated food after cooking, on a cutting board for instance, or a contaminated countertop.

Virtually all food contains organisms that at some point may harm you. But if you handle the food properly by keeping it cold, below 4C, then heating it to an internal temperature of 70C (158F), you would eliminate most of the risks," Idziak said.

Idziak and Judy Campbell, a dietitian at McGill University's School of Dietetics and Human Nutrition, offer these tips …

- Store raw meat, fish and poultry well covered on the bottom shelf to ensure the juices don't drip onto other foods.
- To avoid cross-contamination, store cooked and ready-to-eat foods (such as salads, fruit, cheese and cooked meats) away from raw meat and poultry.
- Never store uncovered food in the fridge. Not only will it dry out, but there's a greater risk of cross-contamination.
- Don't cram. Adequate air circulation is crucial for maintaining the correct temperature throughout the fridge.

- Don't trust your nose. "Meat kept for a week may not smell bad or even look bad, but it may be that the bacteria inside have multiplied enough to cause food poisoning," Campbell said.
- Mustard doesn't last forever. Condiments and sauces with high levels of salt, sugar and vinegar, which prevent bacterial growth, don't perish quickly. But they do go bad. Check expiry dates regularly.
- Eggs should always be stored on a main shelf in their original cartons, not on a door shelf, where the temperature fluctuates.
- Don't leave the door open for long periods of time.
- Clean the inside of the fridge and freezer regularly with baking soda dissolved in warm water or antibacterial cleaner. In older models, defrost regularly to prevent build-up.
- Don't buy perishables in bulk, unless you plan to freeze them.
- When in doubt, throw it out.

Questions

Knowledge and Understanding

1. Find proof in the article that the statement "most people don't take refrigerator hygiene as seriously as they should" is true.

2. Identify the foods most likely to cause food poisoning.

3. What are some of the most common kitchen mistakes that can lead to food poisoning?

Communication

4. A close friend knows that you are taking a food and nutrition course. She has asked you to explain how she can reduce her risk of getting food poisoning. Prepare a dialogue between you and your friend explaining the importance of food safety. Choose five of the tips listed in the article on how to keep the fridge clean and safe, and include these points in your dialogue. Give your friend practical suggestions on how she can stay safe.

Thinking and Inquiry

5. Based on your reading of this article, respond to the following:
   - **a.** What has the reporter done to capture the reader's attention?
   - **b.** Is the coverage informative?
   - **c.** What sources has the reporter cited? In your opinion, are they reliable?

Name: ______________________ Date: __________ Class: __________

Bacteria Busters

W-4

This activity will allow you to determine the presence of bacteria and whether various cleaning products remove or kill the bacteria.

Purpose

To determine which practices will kill or remove surface bacteria.

Materials

Petri dishes
Agar gel*
Cotton swabs
Sterile water
Different cleaning products (antibacterial, sanitizer, cleaner)
Paper towels
Saliva or yogurt

Method

1. Prepare agar gel and fill petri dishes.
2. Moisten cotton swabs by using sterile water and rub moist swab across the surface of your lab table.
3. Carefully open your petri dish and make a large X across the nutrient agar with the cotton swab. Close the lid immediately and label this container "A."
4. Using different cleaning products and paper towels to dry the surface, treat sections of your lab table, each with a different cleaning product. Follow directions provided on individual cleaning products.
5. After treating and drying each section, draw a cotton swab across it and repeat step 3, labelling each container with the type of solution used.
6. Place all the dishes in a warm dark place for five days. Do not open any of the dishes.
7. Carefully follow your teacher's instructions for disposing of the dishes when the project is complete.

Observations

Create a daily data table for each container.

Questions:

1. What do you think will happen in each container?
2. Which products killed or removed the bacteria best?
3. What is the best way to kill or remove surface bacteria?
4. What was the function of dish "A"?

*If agar gel isn't available, prepared instant mashed potatoes in petri dishes can be used instead.

Name: ______________________ Date: __________ Class: __________

W-5

Mouldy Bread

Bread mould is a type of airborne fungus. Once they settle on food, moulds use the food as their own food source. Moulds are not plants, have no chlorophyll, and cannot make their own food.

Purpose

To determine what causes bread to become mouldy.

Materials for each group

Plastic zipper bags
Bread slice
Eye dropper (a straw can be used if droppers are unavailable)
Water
Plastic knife
Paper plate
Masking tape
Markers
Magnifying lens

Procedure

1. Cut the bread slice in half on the plate. Place one half in each bag. Seal one bag and label it Bag A, using the tape and marker.
2. Using the dropper or straw, place 10 drops of water on the second half.
3. Seal and label it Bag B.
4. Place both bags in a warm, dark place for three to five days.

Note: Do not open the bags once they are sealed.
Carefully follow your teacher's directions to discard the bags after the experiment is completed.

Observations

Predict what will happen in each bag.

Draw or write observations each day, using a magnifying lens to look through the bag.

Questions:

1. Where did the mould come from?
2. Why was it important to keep one slice of bread dry?
3. How can you help prevent the bread from getting mouldy?
4. Can you think of any good uses for mould?

Name: ______________________ Date: __________ Class: __________

Food Safety Case Study

W-6

Aaron attended a gathering of his co-workers on a warm July Saturday. The theme was international dining, and he and his wife were asked to bring Argentine style beef, a stew-like dish. They followed the recipe carefully, and took it out of the oven at 1 pm. They kept the dish warm by wrapping the pan in a towel. They drove to the party and set the dish out on the buffet table at 3 pm. Dinner was to be served at 4 pm. However, the guests were enjoying themselves so much that no one began to eat until 6 pm. Aaron made sure he sampled the beef that he and his wife made, while his wife did not. He also had some salad, garlic bread, and a sweet dessert made with coconut.

The couple returned home at 11 pm and went to bed. About 2 am Aaron knew something was wrong. He had severe abdominal pain and had to make a mad dash to the bathroom. For the next three hours he had severe diarrhoea. By dawn, the diarrhoea had subsided and he started to feel better. After a few cups of tea and a light breakfast, he felt like himself by noon.

What type of foodborne illness did Aaron probably contract?

What precautions for avoiding foodborne illness were ignored by Aaron, his wife, and the rest of the people at the party?

Rewrite the scenario so that the party-goers could substantially reduce their risk of foodborne illness.

Name: ______________________ Date: __________ Class: __________

Poster

Using the resources in the classroom, create a small poster that can be used in the classroom foods lab.

Choose one of the following topics:

a) Safe operation of small and large appliances in the foods lab.
b) Personal hygiene.
c) Safe use of knives.
d) Fire prevention.
e) Safe food-handling procedures.
f) Proper dish-washing procedures.
g) Proper food temperatures.
h) Food-handling guidelines.
i) Thawing food safely.
j) Proper food storage (room temperature, refrigerator, freezer).

Criteria for the poster:

- Provide accurate information.
- Determine what is most important. What do we really need to know?
- Present facts neatly.
- Use graphics and other visuals to attract the eye.
- List sources for additional information (web sites, public health etc.)

Safety Poster—Assessment and Evaluation

Criteria	Level 1	Level 2	Level 3	Level 4
Knowledge and Understanding ■ Accurately describe safe kitchen practices. ■ List sources for additional information.				
Thinking and Inquiry ■ Make judgments to determine what information is most relevant.				
Communication ■ Use proper spelling and grammar. ■ Make poster neat and attractive. ■ Use graphics/visuals to highlight topic, attract the eye.				

Additional Resources

Resources for Energy Input and Output

Energy Used (Calories Used During Activity):

Food for Today, First Canadian Edition

- Refer to page 404 for a brief list of activities and calories used per minute.
- NutriStrategy Software—http://www.nutristrategy.com/activitylist.htm
- Lists calories burned during exercise for a range of exercises.
- Lists data for three different weights.

Caloriesperhour.com—http://www.caloriesperhour.com/

- Has information for many activities (various ranges from sedentary to fully active).
- Also has details on some nutrients for common foods.

Fitresource—Your Health and Fitness Resource—http://www.fitresource.com/Fitness/CalBurn.htm

- Provides information about calories burned for some activities.

West Virginia Dietetic Association—http://www.wvda.org/calcs/gym.html

- Provides information about calories burned for some activities.

Diet Site—online dietitians serving your nutritional needs—http://www.dietsite.com/dt/nutr/file-firsttime.asp

- Allows you to look for specific foods and gives the macronutrient breakdown.
- You need to register to be able to get into analysis.
- Provides exercise tracking.

Energy Consumed (Calories Taken In):

Food for Today, First Canadian Edition

- Refer to page 596 for a brief list of DRIs of some nutrients.

Dietary Reference Intakes—http://www.nal.usda.gov/fnic/etext/000105.html#q5

- Shows dietary reference intakes of elements (minerals), vitamins, and macronutrients.

Nutrient Values of Some Common Foods—http://www.hc-sc.gc.ca/food-aliment/ns-sc/nr-rn/surveillance/e_nutrient_value_of_some_common_.html

- Available in booklet form or free from the above web site (in pdf format).
- Has charted information for most foods.

Diet Site—online dietitians serving your nutritional needs—http://www.dietsite.com/dt/nutr/file-firsttime.asp

- Allows you to look for specific foods and gives the macronutrient breakdown.
- You need to register to be able to get into analysis.
- Provides exercise tracking.

Nutrition Data Website—http://www.nutritiondata.com/index.html

- Allows you to look for specific foods or from categories.
- Shows percentage of calories from fat, carb and protein (and visually too through a pyramid format).
- Also has nutrition facts for each food.
- Information about the nutrients divided into their nutrient categories.
- Provides a chart of nutrient density.
- Provides info about fast-food restaurants.
- Shows American information.

Food Focus and other computer programs

- Program that allows users to input foods and view their nutrients.
- Can be calculated on additional foods.
- A more recent version also takes activity into account.

Nutrient Facts Labels

- Nutrient fact labels are now mandatory in Canada; however, companies are given a grace period to put them in place until 2006.
- Many labels contain information, but it may not be in the standard format yet and/or it may contain more or less information .
- Some foods don't require a label (including fresh fruits and vegetables, meats, fish, and poultry, and alcohol).
- It also contains this information for the serving sizes
- Fast-food restaurants will give out fact sheets upon request.

DRIs for Adolescent Males and Females

14–18 years of age

- UL = the maximum daily level of nutrient intake that is like to pose no risk or adverse effects.
- ND = for some nutrients, there is not enough data to establish a UL.
- Micrograms = µg
- Milligrams = mg
- AMDR = acceptable macronutrient distribution range: the range of intake for the energy source that is associated with reduced risk of chronic disease while providing essential nutrients.

Nutrient	Notes	Measure	Males	Females	UL*
Macronutrients					
Carbohydrate		AMDR*	45–65		
Fibre		Grams	38	26	
Fat	* best to stay under 30%	AMDR	25–35	25–35	
Protein		AMDR	10–30 (52 g)	10–30 (46 g)	
Vitamins					
Fat Soluble					
A	1RAE =1 µg	µg	900	700	2800
D		µg	5	5	50
E		mg	15	15	800
K		µg	75	75	ND
Water Soluble					
C		mg	75	65	1800
B_1 = thiamine		mg	1.2	1.0	ND
B_2 = riboflavin		mg	1.3	1.0	ND
Niacin	1NE =1 mg	mg	16	14	30
Folate = folic acid	1DFE = 1µg	µg	400	400	800
Biotin		µg	25	25	ND
Pantothenic acid		mg	5	5	ND
B_6		mg	1.3	1.3	80
B_{12}		µg	2.4	2.4	ND
Minerals					
Calcium		mg	1300	1300	2500
Copper		µg	890	890	8000
Fluoride		mg	3	3	10
Iodine		µg	150	150	900
Iron		mg	11	15	45
Magnesium		mg	410	360	
Manganese		mg	2.2	1.6	
Phosphorus		mg	1250	1250	4000
Zinc		mg	11	9	34

(Source: *Dietary Reference Intakes* at: http://www.nal.usda.gov/fnic/etext/000105.html#q5. Retrieved May 17, 2004.)

Reference 3

Micro-Nutrients (no energy)											
Minerals					Vitamins						
Calcium m g	Iron mg	Zing mg	Sodium mg	Potassium mg	A IU	C mg	B6 mg	Folate mg	Thiamin mg	Riboflavin mg	Niacin NE

Micro-Nutrients (no energy)											
Minerals					Vitamins						
Calcium m g	Iron mg	Zing mg	Sodium mg	Potassium mg	A IU	C mg	B6 mg	Folate mg	Thiamin mg	Riboflavin mg	Niacin NE

Credits

33 News Release: "Canada's Food Guide to Healthy Eating to Undergo an Update," Health Canada, March 10, 2004. Reproduced with the permission of the Minister of Public Works and Government Services Canada, 2004; **63** Table: Kraft Canada, Dairy Farmers of Canada and Dietitians of Canada. *2003 Report on Healthy Eating Challenges Facing Women*. Produced by the Dietitians of Canada. © March 2003; **74** Article: "Teen girls get less nutrients than boys," October 25, 2000. *The Canadian Press*; **116** Article: "Conscientious chocolate" by Jennifer Bain, *The Toronto Star*, April 7, 2004. Reprinted with permission - Torstar Syndication Services; **142** Ice Cream. Source: "Finding Science in Ice Cream—An Experiment for Secondary School Classrooms," http://www.foodsci.uoguelph.ca/dairyedu/findsci.html. Retrieved July 5, 2004; **160** Food Packaging Technology. Source: *Careers in a Package*, Packaging Careers Council of Canada, http://www.packagingcareers.org. Retrieved July 6, 2004 **199** Adapted from "Rules to keep fridge clean and safe" by Susan Semenak. Copyright © CanWest Global Communication Corp. 2004. All rights reserved.